Diane Clement

AT THE TOMATO

ALSO BY DIANE CLEMENT

Chef on the Run (1982)

More Chef on the Run (1984)

Chef and Doctor on the Run (1986)

Fresh Chef on the Run (1990)

Diane Clement

AT THE TOMATO

Recipes and Tales from the Tomato Fresh Food Café

Illustrations by Ken MacDonald

RAINCOAST BOOKS

Vancouver

First published in 1995 by
Raincoast Book Distribution Ltd.
8680 Cambie Street
Vancouver, B.C.
V6P 6M9
(604) 323-7100

CANADIAN CATALOGUING IN PUBLICATION DATA

Clement, Diane, 1936-
Diane Clement at the Tomato

Includes index.
ISBN 1-895714-95-8

1. Cookery. 2. Tomato Fresh Food Café. I. Title. II. Title: At the Tomato.
TX714.C63 1995   641.5   C95-910368-6

Designed by Dean Allen
Project Editor: Michael Carroll
Copy Editor: Rachelle Kanefsky
Cover Photography by Kharen Hill

Printed and bound in Canada

To Jennifer, the best daughter and partner a mother could have; to Jamie, our talented, creative partner and friend; to Haik, our big-hearted friend and partner; to my family, Doug, Rand, and Suzanne, for always being there; to my wild, upbeat Tomato team, my second family; and to our dedicated customers, the spirit and life of the Tomato. You have all made my Tomato journey a joy.

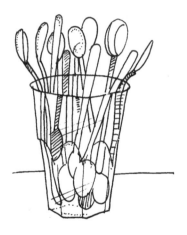

Contents

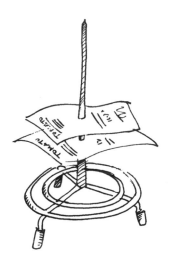

Acknowledgements

A SPECIAL THANKS goes out to the following for their support and faith in the Tomato Fresh Food Café: David Matheson, my loving twin brother and our brilliant legal adviser; Glenys Morgan, the backbone of the Tomato; Devine Elden, the Tomato's guardian angel; Jack Harrison, our Tomato Patriarch; Helen Nachtigal and Jeto Hundal, for their enthusiasm, help, and friendship; Marcelle McLean, our special friend and first manager of Tomato-to-Go; Mac and Betty Jane Norris, for their enthusiasm for our Tomato dream; and Jean Robinson, Mary Henderson, and Boby Luckacs, true Tomato pals.

I would also like to thank Ken MacDonald, extraordinary graphic artist and stage designer; Morris Panych, genius writer, actor, and one of the original Tomato pals; Heather Nichol, talented, dynamic artist, responsible for the artwork on the chef's jacket worn on the cover of this book; Vi Cross, our caring expert accountant; John MacLaren, our patient Tomato computer and bookkeeping whiz; Jamie Madill, for his expert advice at all times; Ingo Grady, our wine advisor and friend; the Honourable Senator Ray Perrault, for his enthusiasm and love of tomatoes; Les Dames d'Escoffier, our dynamic overachiever team; *Much West*'s Terry David Mulligan and his wife Peggy, for their tremendous support and friendship; BCTV's Saturday morning *Cooking Show*; the CBC and the vibrant Vicki Gabereau; *B.C. Home* and *Western Living* magazines; the dynamic B.C. Hot House team; the Tomato's suppliers, one and all; and, finally, the patient, talented Raincoast Books team. I love you all.

Introduction

"WHY DON'T YOU WORK in a restaurant for a few months before you make a final decision on opening a place of your own?" Doug, my husband, suggested to our daughter Jennifer, Jamie Norris, our partner, and me.

In retrospect Doug's suggestion was wise. But if we had taken his advice, I honestly don't think we would have ever opened a restaurant of our own in Vancouver. And just think of all the challenges and fun we would have missed!

How did we start? First, Jennifer, who's an actor, and Jamie, who's a playwright, casually said one day that they were thinking of looking into setting up a hot dog stand at Stanley Park. This was intended as a secondary challenge, something to do along with their acting and writing. Sometime later we were all sitting around the kitchen table in the evening when Jennifer said, "Why don't we open a little juice and cappuccino bar with your homecooking, Mom? It could be a riot. And I know the perfect spot. That old landmark diner at Cambie and 17th."

Originally the café was called the Rosebud. It opened in 1947 and operated as a chop house, eventually evolving into a coffee shop, then a Chinese-Canadian food diner called the Sun Ray Café that was known for great burgers in the late 1980s.

Next, a dear friend of ours, Jack Harrison, came on the scene. Over a cup of tea he asked if we had found a location for our restaurant, and I mentioned the place on Cambie and 17th. Jack, a former Vancouver policeman who always has his ear to the ground, said, "Diane, would you believe it? I get my hair cut at Charlie's, the barber next door to the restaurant you want. Let me do some scouting for you. I do know it's pretty greasy and neglected and that nobody goes there anymore."

Two days later Jack called and said, "I've got the scoop. Their lease will be listed in the papers in 4 days, so you'd better get moving." On May 15, 1991, 3 days after Jack called, we signed the lease.

Jack is now 85 years old and has officially been named the Patriarch of the Tomato Fresh Food Café. He drops in weekly to have his hair cut by Charlie and to have a quick chat with us over a cup of coffee and his favourite sweet of the day.

Well, back then, in 1991, we had a restaurant, but the only person with any experience was Jennifer, who had worked in a cappuccino bar and a kitchen shop while attending university. We felt we needed a fourth partner, and so Haik Gharibians, who has a passion for cooking and entertaining, came on board. Haik, an acclaimed physio-therapist with the American Olympic Figure Skating Team and the Canadian Olympic Swim Team, had no idea he would soon be spending his weekends in the Tomato kitchen "chopping" forever.

So, there were now 4 inexperienced lovers of food embarking on the opening of a new café. First question: Where to start? Answer, another question: What should we call our café?

A good, catchy name is crucial. We had a lot of fun try-ing to make a decision, but it was difficult to come up with something we could all agree on. One afternoon in the main Vancouver Public Library we came across a picture of a café in Chicago called Scoozi's, which had a giant tomato over its front door. Somehow this image of a bright, vibrant, ripe, juicy, almost voluptuous fruit symbolized everything we envisioned for our diner. The name of the fruit then led us to design and colour ideas, and we knew we had something we could all fly with. Besides, all four of us loved tomatoes!

Next, we needed a business plan. That led to a lot of new questions. How do we find the best suppliers? How much do we order at a time? Will the suppliers give us credit? Do they deliver? Where do we find good equipment? How do we know secondhand equipment won't break down? We were beginning to have dreams of tons of food arriving at the back door in the pouring rain while our dishwashers exploded.

But Jen was amazing. She took on the challenge, which was great, because when it comes to business, I'm hopeless. Right off the mark I told Jen, "Put me in the kitchen and I'll be as happy as a clam. Two things I don't want to do are cash and coffee." Jen knows me well. She always keeps me on track when I start to stray away from controlling high food costs.

Jennifer went to the library to find everything she could on opening a business, while Jamie proceeded to renovate the café. Before long Doug joined Jamie, along with a committed battalion of family, friends, athletes, actors, and tradespeople, and got down to the "fun." Our first task was a massive weeklong cleaning marathon. Tidying up the basement was comparable to going on an archaeological dig. Truckloads of junk were hauled away and, honestly, there must have been at least 10 trips just to get rid of pots of grease. I vowed I would never, ever install a deep fryer.

After a few weeks of working around the clock, our little café finally took shape. Jamie's brilliant artistic talents brought the place alive with bright yellow and red walls that complemented the reupholstered booths and the black, grey, and red squares of the tile flooring. He had captured the old-diner atmosphere with a New Age feeling. The café was funky, cheerful, and warm.

In the midst of all this chaos our prospective Tomato customers began to appear. Every day people would drop by and say things like: "Welcome to our neighbourhood. Wow! A juice bar. Great!" Dane DeViller and Sean Hoisein were the very first neighbours to come by, and to this day they will always be our number one customers. Brent and Maureen Cameron and their daughter Ilana, who eventually did our first menus on her computer, would also drop by daily from their Wonder Tree School.

We had arrived! It was really going to happen. In a few days our doors would open for the first time.

Doug, ever-cautious, asked me back then, "Diane, do you really want to 'entertain' 250 people daily? Are you ready for that?" Those questions still haunt me today. Entertaining has always been easy for me. I love sitting around the table enjoying food that I've prepared for family and friends, sipping new wines, discussing everything from Olympic performances to the latest great play in town, or debating whatever comes to mind. So the challenge for me was to create a similar atmosphere in a restaurant: prepare food for our customers just as their mothers would do if they had the time.

Since I'm quite competitive, I rose to the challenge. But was Doug ever right! Obviously, running a restaurant isn't the same as entertaining at home. Instead of making soup for a dozen people or preparing a buffet for 50 or so, I now had to whip up monstrous proportions – enough food for 250 hungry customers every single day.

Weeks before opening I developed new recipes on a much grander scale, in addition to adapting my all-time classics. It was important for me to serve what we at the Tomato like to describe as "healthful" food. Doug and I wrote a bestselling cookbook entitled *Chef and Doctor on the Run,* which incorporated the healthy lifestyle principles we still live by. And I believe the menu at the Tomato reflects our belief that we all must strive to eat less fat, sugar, and salt, as well as exercise regularly. We also strive at the Tomato to meet the requirements of special diets. More and more people are eating less or no meat, so we offer many vegetarian dishes, lots of salads, and plenty of hearty grain breads. Spices from around the world are also part of the Tomato repertoire, and we shy away from processed or pre-mixed foods. We believe in making everything from scratch, with no preservatives. Our food is wholesome, although we do have yummy desserts for those who wish to indulge.

Well, the real shock came when we finally opened for business on August 22, 1991. I'll never forget that first day. At 9:00 a.m. the restaurant was full. With Jamie and Jennifer in the front and myself and Susan Hansen, a newly graduated student from Dubrulle French Culinary School, spearheading the kitchen, we were in business.

The orders came fast and furious. Two omelettes in a bread bed with a side of sausage and bacon. Three hard-boiled eggs, 2 medium, 1 soft. Four waffle plates, 3 orders of multigrained toast, and a side of hash browns. On and on it went. Never having worked in a restaurant before, I took one look at all the orders and thought, What am I doing here? I must be crazy. Is this supposed to be fun? My bones ached, I lost my voice, and I soon had burns up and down my arms from the hot grill, as well as raccoon circles under my eyes from 16 hours of sleepless preparation for the opening.

When the clock finally read 4:30 and we put up the CLOSED sign, I thought, This is harder than training for the Olympics or running a marathon. We had all experienced a day in the life of the crazy restaurant frenzy. Six months later we got our wine and beer licence and then extended our hours to 10:00 p.m. Six months after that, when the space next door became available, we opened the Tomato-to-Go. Offering our delicious take-out baking and catering, the Tomato-to-Go caught on quickly.

Now, after 4 years, it's hard to believe we survived, let alone that our Tomato team has grown from 4 to 30 people. To date more than 200 people have worked with us at the Tomato. This hectic business has many ups and downs, just like life itself, but the rewards far outweigh whatever frustrations might arise. There is a certain satisfaction in having customers tell me things like: "We love your food. Thanks for the recipe for your Whole Wheat Loaf. I make it all the time. And that banana bread reminds me of my mom's." Or "Keep making that Indonesian Squash Soup. It's the ultimate. We sure love your friendly atmosphere."

Yes, it's been a challenge, and as I wander through the restaurant greeting new and regular customers, or take time to sit in a booth and enjoy a meal, I still can't quite believe this place is really ours. During times of frustration or exhaustion, I often draw on the lessons I've learned as an athlete, coach, and administrator. Winning and losing are part of everyday life. When I have to deal with staff problems, I remember what one of my Olympic coaches used as his philosophy: "No matter what you do in dealing with people in business or in coaching situations, you should always be close enough to be a friend but distant enough to be a leader."

For me the most important creed is to have respect for every person you come into contact with, and expect the same in return. I have used the principles that sports have taught me. At the Tomato it is the total team effort that wins in the end. There are no stars at our café. Everyone is a key player.

I've written 4 bestselling cookbooks with Jack and Liz Bryan, and it was a joy working with such talented friends. But I feel that telling the story and revealing the secrets and recipes of the Tomato Fresh Food Café with Raincoast has been just as exciting and fun. And what a story! Here you'll find out what we put in that comforting potato salad and what makes our corn bread so moist. And you'll discover whether or not we put real espresso in our chocolate cheesecake. From now on there will be no more guessing. We reveal everything just for you because, ultimately, it is people who have allowed the Tomato to grow and mature and become a meeting place to enjoy good food with friends. We think every restaurant should strive to be a home away from home. That's what I like to think the Tomato is, and if you can't get down to check it out in person, then please enjoy the good eating you'll find in this book.

Brunch
Bunch
Specials

Golden Buttermilk Pancakes

The most requested Sunday blue plate specials are pancakes and French toast. "I keep multiplying this recipe every Sunday but we still run out," Sue Godin comments, as she quickly whips up yet another batch. Our regulars love her surprise toppings along with real Québec maple syrup. Makes about 18 4-inch (10-cm) medium pancakes.

2 cups (500 ml) ALL-PURPOSE FLOUR

1 teaspoon (5 ml) BAKING SODA

pinch of SALT

2 tablespoons (30 ml) WHITE SUGAR

2 large EGGS, slightly beaten

2 cups (500 ml) BUTTERMILK

2 tablespoons (30 ml) MELTED BUTTER

Combine the dry ingredients in a bowl. Add the eggs, buttermilk, and melted butter and stir only until the flour is barely moistened. Batter will have a few lumps. Let sit for at least 30 minutes. Have ready a lightly greased hot griddle or sauté pan.

For uniform pancakes, use a ¼ cup (60 ml) measure, pour onto the skillet and grill until bubbles begin, about 2 minutes. Flip over and grill until golden brown, about 2 minutes more. Pancakes should be golden on both sides.

Special treat: When blueberries are at their peak, add 1 cup (250 ml) to the batter.

The first private birthday party held at the Tomato, on September 12, 1991, was in honour of Elisa Lloyd-Smith when she turned nine. Her chosen menu was Pissaladiere, the French version of pizza, Caesar salad, Old-fashioned Chocolate Cake, and ice cream. Her delightful friends joined us in the kitchen to make the pizza, and to get the inside scoop on a restaurant kitchen, along with theatrical antics from Jamie, Jennifer, and our actor/chef, Jimmy Tate.

Classic Tomato
French Toast

This is my old standby that our children grew up on and our Tomato pals devour in minutes. Serves 4, allowing 8 pieces of bread. Double recipe for a hungry crew.

In a large shallow bowl, whisk about ⅔ cup (160 ml) of WHOLE MILK with 5 beaten EGGS. Add 1 teaspoon (5 ml) VANILLA, ¼ teaspoon (1 ml) CINNAMON, a good pinch of NUTMEG, and 3 to 4 teaspoons (15 to 20 ml) WHITE SUGAR. Cut day-old BREAD into ½-inch (12-mm) thick slices and put into the egg mixture, soaking each piece well. Let sit at least 30 minutes, covered.

Melt about 2 to 4 tablespoons (45 to 60 ml) of UNSALT-ED BUTTER in a skillet and sauté the soaked sourdough or French bread over medium heat until golden, then flip over and cook the other side. Serve immediately. If you are doing a large batch, cover the toast with foil and keep warm in the oven at a low temperature.

To serve: Sprinkle with icing sugar and offer a variety of sauces, jams, and maple syrup.

Note: Try raisin-cinnamon bread or croissants, cut in half, for a change from the traditional.

Al's Brie Strawberry French Toast

Chef Allan's creation is sensational; what else can I say? Prepare the classic French toast batter based on 8 slices of bread. Serves 6 to 8.

Cut the SOURDOUGH or FRENCH BREAD into ½-inch (12-mm) slices. Then cut across, almost through, forming a pocket. Spread an even ¼-inch (6-mm) layer of thick BRIE across the pocket, then an even layer of thinly sliced strawberries. Press down lightly. These can be prepared in advance.

Just before serving: Soak each piece in the egg mixture, coating well. Grill or melt a little butter in a skillet and cook on each side until golden and slightly crispy. Serve immediately with maple syrup and fresh sliced strawberries. Good with a strawberry purée as well.

TOPPINGS FOR PANCAKES OR FRENCH TOAST

Fresh Peach Yogurt Sauce

Try this when the peaches are at their sweetest and juiciest! Serves 4.

1 pint (0.5 *l*) PEACH YOGURT, or ½ pint (0.25 *l*)
PEACH to ½ pint (0.25 *l*) VANILLA YOGURT

4 to 5 PEACHES, peeled and sliced

½ teaspoon (2.5 ml) VANILLA

Combine and refrigerate. Best made just before serving.

When we first opened, Marc Preston, a music critic, practically lived at the Tomato. He occupied the corner barstool nearest the kitchen and ate his way through our whole menu. Finally, one day, he asked, "Do you think I could work here? I love it so much." Marc is now one of our managers, still writes, and is a true-blue Tomato pal.

Fried Apples

Serves 4. In a skillet, melt 3 tablespoons (45 ml) of BUTTER. Add 4 Granny Smith, Newton, or Gala APPLES, cored and cut into eighths. Sauté about 5 minutes. Sprinkle over 2 tablespoons (30 ml) of BROWN SUGAR, 1 teaspoon (5 ml) of CINNAMON, and a ½ cup (125 ml) of APPLE JUICE and continue to cook for about 10 minutes, or until the apples are soft. Serve warm. Can be made in advance and reheated.

Louisiana Style Pancakes *or* French Toast

A popular topping with a southern flare. In the French toast batter try substituting half the milk with concentrated orange juice. Makes enough for 4 servings.

In a skillet, melt 3 tablespoons (45 ml) of BUTTER. Add 3 BANANAS, peeled and sliced lengthwise, then cut in half. Sauté for a few minutes, then add 2 to 3 tablespoons (30 to 45 ml) of BROWN SUGAR and a dash of WHITE RUM, ORANGE LIQUEUR, or ORANGE JUICE. Simmer for a minute or 2 to caramelize.

Herb Omelette in *Bed*

"A bread-wedge bed to be exact, filled with a Parmesan Reggiano, 3-egg omelette of roasted peppers, and fresh herbs." That is how our menu describes our unique omelette presentation. Served with our famous hand-cut country style grilled potatoes and grilled lean European bacon (or low-fat turkey sausages) for that extra hungry customer.

At the Tomato, we use a special Armenian flat bread that we slice lengthwise, heat, and fill. Croissants, brioche, or French bread rolls would also do nicely. Cut in half and heat in oven while preparing the omelette. Serves 2 people, based on a 3-egg omelette.

6 extra-large EGGS, or 7 large

2 tablespoons (30 ml) WATER

2 tablespoons (30 ml) canned ROASTED PEPPERS, chopped

2 tablespoons (30 ml) freshly grated PARMESAN CHEESE

1 tablespoon (15 ml) mixed fresh BASIL and DILL

1 tablespoon (15 ml) BUTTER

pinch of PEPPER and SALT

4 pieces of BREAD or ROLLS

Just before serving: Whisk the eggs and water slightly, don't overbeat. Melt the butter in a skillet and add the eggs. Stir for just a second with a spatula. Let the omelette cook, lifting the eggs here and there to let the liquid run underneath for a minute or so. Add the peppers, Parmesan cheese, and herbs, lifting the eggs slightly until they are cooked but still creamy. Add the pepper and salt. If you are folding the omelette, bring the left half to the centre while the centre is soft, but make the third fold as you slide it out onto the bread or roll.

OMELETTE VARIATIONS: Our Mexican or Italian Egg Scramble, featured in our weekend brunch specials, are a huge hit.

I've always had a desire to be a singer, but alas, with a voice like mine, what hope is there? I originally came from the Maritimes and used to say, "Anne Murray went to Las Vegas and I went to the Olympics, but I'd love to switch places just once." I figured she could run the 100-metre dash and I'd do her stage show. At the Tomato my staff have no choice but to listen and laugh when I break out with "Bird on a Wire" or an old Broadway show tune. In days gone by Allan Morgan and John McKinstry would patiently sing along with me as the lunch crowd peered into the kitchen to see if we'd gone totally mad. Then the waiters would join in, and sometimes the customers would pick up a line or two. Other times Bonnie Panych would start the staff lattes going as we broke out with "It's Caffe Latte Time" while dancing the cancan. Those were the days!

Mexican Egg Scramble

For 2 people use the basic omelette mixture of:

6 extra-large or 7 large EGGS, plus 2 tablespoons (30 ml)
of WATER, whisked

2 tablespoons (30 ml) canned mild GREEN CHILI
PEPPERS, chopped

3 tablespoons (45 ml) MONTEREY JACK CHEESE, grated

2 tablespoons (30 ml) fresh CILANTRO, chopped (optional)

pinch of PEPPER and SALT

1 tablespoon (15 ml) BUTTER

2 10-inch (25-cm) flour or whole wheat TORTILLAS

1 cup (250 ml) TOMATO SALSA

6 tablespoons (90 ml) old CHEDDAR CHEESE, grated

Just before serving: Heat the tortillas in foil in a 350° F (180° C) oven for about 5 minutes, or grill them on both sides.

In a skillet, heat the butter and add the egg and water mixture. With a spatula, stir slightly to cook the eggs, adding the green chili peppers, Monterey Jack cheese, and cilantro. Stir gently to scramble. Add the pepper and salt to taste.

Place in 2 small ramekins, top with about 2 to 3 tablespoons (30 to 45 ml) salsa, then about 3 tablespoons (45 ml) cheddar cheese. Place under the grill or salamander until the cheese has melted. Top with a sprig of cilantro. Serve the tortillas cut into triangles and placed around the ramekins.

Did you know that the original French name for the tomato was *pomme d'amour,* or love apple? Maybe it got that name because red is the colour of love. Or is it an aphrodisiac?

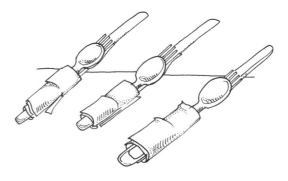

Italian Egg *Scramble*

Instead of the Mexican touch, substitute the following to the basic egg and water mixture for 2:

2 tablespoons (30 ml) ASIAGO or
freshly grated PARMESAN CHEESE

2 tablespoons (30 ml) FONTINA
or MONTEREY JACK CHEESE

2 tablespoons (30 ml) canned ROASTED PEPPERS, chopped

2 tablespoons (30 ml) fresh BASIL, chopped

PEPPER and SALT to taste

2 pieces FOCACCIA BREAD

To serve: Follow directions for the Mexican Scramble, place in ramekins, top with a sprig of basil, and serve with warmed focaccia bread.

Note: At the Tomato we serve all our omelettes and egg scrambles with a side of hand-cut hash brown potatoes.

The Tomato's Grilled Country Style Potatoes

The Tomato secrets to our breakfast potatoes are: We allow about ¾ cup (180 ml) per person. We use only the small red or white potatoes, hand cut into 4 to 6 ½ inch (12 mm) cubes. Either on our grill, or in a heavy skillet, we melt a little butter with a little salad oil just to coat the grill or skillet. We then add the potatoes, along with some chopped white or red onions. How many? Your call. Sauté the potatoes and onions until they have a slightly crusty finish. Add pepper to taste and a pinch of salt. That's it, no more, no less, but they are homecooking at its best. They can also be kept warm in the oven while you prepare the eggs.

B.C. Hot House and I have joined forces to promote their tomatoes, cucumbers, lettuce, and peppers. The campaign, called Juicy Secrets, was a huge success. It won their company, the Western Greenhouse Growers Cooperative Association, the American Marketing Association Award for the best marketing promotions in British Columbia in 1994. My recipes and "juicy secrets" found their way to the supermarkets as part of their advertising campaign. It was fun to be part of this successful campaign for products that I strongly endorse and enjoy serving at the Tomato.

Fresh *Squeeze* Juice Bar

JUICE BARS ARE definitely "in," with every fresh fruit and vegetable combination imaginable. How do you start at home?

What I would suggest if you are keen on joining the Juice Bar Club is to pick up a current book on juicing. Most health food stores have information on the best juicers and how to start.

One of the highest priorities for us when we opened the Tomato was to have the first restaurant juice bar in Vancouver, which we did. Many have since followed our trend and its popularity is ever growing. We had a lot of fun coming up with the juice concoctions and names for them. From day one, our juice bar has been a success. It has a personality all its own. We started off with the Champion Juicer then graduated to a larger, more powerful commercial model. Here are a few of our potions:

Susi Q

Topping the charts, the all-time favourite is the Susi Q, named in honour of our daughter-in-law, Suzanne. Strawberries, oranges, and bananas are the winning trio.

In your juicer or blender, combine:

1 ripe BANANA, peeled of course

4 to 5 STRAWBERRIES, fresh or frozen

2 cups (500 ml) fresh squeezed ORANGE JUICE

Heavenly Cleanse

Ranked no. 2 is the Heavenly Cleanse. It does have a rather purifying effect as you drink this tangy, interesting combination. You really believe that colds will be gone forever if you treat yourself daily to this potent drink.

The drama begins at the Tomato fountain with the roar of the juice machine as carrots, apples, ginger, and lemons are pushed through the funnel to create the first juice order of the day – a Heavenly Cleanse for someone at the counter. The stars at centre stage are the Tomato juicers, who perform daily for customers eager for that special juice concoction. We opened the restaurant with Thomas, our New Age health guru, then came artist Dan the Man, Mr. Personality, and bubbly Kat, the Queen of the Juice Bar. Today, on any given day, the orders keep pouring in: "Small Veg Head, Popeye's Potion, and 2 large Gone Gorillas for the cyclists on four. Small Susi Q for the baby on three. Need a Whammy for Steve, who had a big night and needs something to get him through the day." And the beet goes on!

juice of 2 peeled, cored APPLES

3 medium CARROTS, unpeeled, roots chopped

1 tablespoon (15 ml) fresh GINGER JUICE

juice of ½ LEMON

Whammy

A tropical paradise!

1 ripe BANANA

1 cup (250 ml) fresh squeezed ORANGE JUICE

1 cup (250 ml) fresh PINEAPPLE JUICE

Angel's Aperitif

Named after our good friend Devine and the
Tomato's guardian angel.

3 medium APPLES, peeled and cored

1 tablespoon (15 ml) fresh GINGER JUICE

2 tablespoons (30 ml) fresh BEET JUICE

Actually owning a cappuccino
machine was a big kick for
Jamie. Now he could have a
caffe latte whenever he wanted
one. Fortunately he discovered
that it's not a great idea to drink
7 or 8 lattes every single day.
Unfortunately it took him 2 ½
years to figure that out. We've
always served our lattes in local
potter Suzy Birstein's colourful
ceramic bowls.

Daytripper

When you're off and running, this will make your day!

1 cup (250 ml) fresh APPLE JUICE

1 cup (250 ml) fresh PINEAPPLE JUICE

4 to 5 strawberries, FRESH OR FROZEN

Gone Gorilla

For the wildness in all of us, go for it!

1 ripe BANANA, what else?

2 cups (500 ml) fresh PINEAPPLE JUICE

Veg Head

Healthy drinking at its ultimate!

2 to 3 inches (5 to 7.5 cm) of an
unpeeled ENGLISH CUCUMBER
4 medium CARROTS, roots chopped
2 CELERY STALKS
1 tablespoon (15 ml) fresh BEET JUICE
tablespoons (30 ml) fresh SPINACH JUICE

The Georgia Straight food critic Angela Murrills wrote the following about our Juice Bar: "When you belly up to the bar at the Tomato and order a fresh-squeezed juice, the subtext to the high-level buzz of conversation is the chain-saw noise of the juicer and the whirl of the blender, which may say 'margaritas' to you, but here it means 1 of 20 harmonious marriages of fruit and vegetable juices. A big 14-ounce hit of Veg Head, and just to look at the tall glass topped with its swirls of dark green [spinach and celery], deep orange [carrot], and ruby-coloured [beet] froth, is enough to send the red corpuscles surging around your body, cranking your metabolism into overdrive."

Popeye's Potion

Olive Oyl would have loved this magic blend!

4 medium CARROTS, roots chopped
2 CELERY STALKS
2 tablespoons (30 ml) fresh SPINACH JUICE

The Fitness Group Smoothie

It's my jump start for the day! Add a perfect Fitness Group workout, and a new day begins. Look out!
Throw the following in a blender:

½ cup (125 ml) SKIM MILK
½ cup (125 ml) plain or vanilla YOGURT
1 tablespoon (15 ml) WHEAT GERM
1 teaspoon (5 ml) VANILLA
½ ripe BANANA
1 cup (250 ml) fresh or frozen STRAWBERRIES
3 ICE CUBES (only if fruit is fresh)

Blend at high speed for a few seconds.

Marc's Magic Lemonade

Marc Preston makes a presence as our day manager. In real life he is a successful rock music critic. He has his fans who not only adore him, but love his lemonade as well.

4 cups (1 *l*) HOT WATER

1 tea bag, FENNEL HERB TEA

¾ cup (180 ml) SUGAR

juice of 6 LEMONS

Add the tea bag to the hot water, brew for 15 minutes, add the sugar, and stir until dissolved. Strain the lemon juice (to remove pulp) into the brewed tea. Add more lemon for a tarter drink. Pour over lots of ice.

Kat's Scrumptious Strawberry Lemonade

Kat Ruosso is the Queen of the Juice Bar. She is one of our longest-serving employees. We are all so proud of Kat. This year she received her diploma from the Vancouver Vocational Institute as an aspiring chef. Our customers adore her – with her charm, quick wit, wild hats, and bubbly personality, they look forward to having her whip up their favourite Kat Special. She has been great filling in for my staff at Tomato-to-Go whenever someone is sick or has another commitment. She is a total winner and we wish her every success.

8 cups (2 *l*) WATER

juice of 11 LEMONS

½ cup (125 ml) HONEY, blended
with ½ cup (125 ml) HOT WATER

½ cup (125 ml) frozen whole STRAWBERRIES

Mix the water and lemon juice in a large pitcher. Set aside. In a blender, combine the honey mixture with the strawberries, blend until smooth. Add to the lemon water, mix well. Add more honey or lemon to taste. Chill. Serve in large goblets with a lot of ice and a twist of lemon.

One busy Saturday morning when we were just getting the hang of our new juice machine, we all watched in horror as it shot an orange across the restaurant and into the opposite wall, narrowly missing a gentleman's head. Someone once told Jamie that this particular juice machine was actually designed by an ex-employee of Boeing, but we've never been able to confirm that.

Soup's On!

ONE OF THE first shocks of starting a restaurant business came when I began to prepare a soup for our opening. Having to jump from preparing soups for 25 to 30 cooking students to over 250 customers a day was an eye-opener. I thought, How can we sell this giant pot of soup? It will last for days. Well, it all disappeared in a few hours. We now have 2 of the biggest stockpots we could find, full to the brim with new soups daily.

Before tackling homemade soups, invest in a good quality stockpot from a speciality kitchen shop. I would recommend you start with a 12-quart (13-*l*) stockpot. Most soups freeze well, so go for a big batch of soup while you're at it. I like to freeze the soup in small containers, enough for 2 to 4 servings for easy and quick thawing.

"Good morning. What's your soup special today?" "New Mexico Corn Chowder and Indonesian Squash," I reply. "We'll be right over." We have our faithful soup fans that drop by for our daily specials with a basket of our country breads to soak up the last drop. Our talented chefs continue to surprise us with unusual flavour combinations from around the world. It is difficult to give the specific amounts of ingredients for a soup recipe because you just keep adding more vegetable stock and spices as you go along to reach the right thickness and taste. These are merely rough guidelines for you to take up the challenge and create your own masterpiece soups! The secret, as I tell all my chefs, is to taste, taste, and taste again! I always ask, "Does it have an *identity*?"

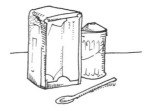

Indonesian Squash *Soup*

This is an adaptation of a recipe I had tried years ago, then played around with to come up with our Tomato version. We opened the Tomato with it and still continue to get raves. The flavours come alive with the Indonesian spices, fresh ginger, and lime juice to balance the sweetness of the butternut squash. Serves 10 to 12.

1 ½ tablespoons (22 ml) CORIANDER SEEDS

1 ½ tablespoons (22 ml) TURMERIC

1 ½ tablespoons (22 ml) ground CUMIN

1 ½ tablespoons (22 ml) MADRAS CURRY POWDER

¼ teaspoon (1 ml) dried RED CHILI PEPPER FLAKES

In a mini chopper, grind the coriander seeds, then blend with the rest of the spices. Set aside.

3 tablespoons (45 ml) OLIVE or CANOLA OIL

4 medium white ONIONS, coarsely chopped

6 cloves GARLIC, finely chopped

3 tablespoons (45 ml) fresh GINGER, grated or minced in mini chopper

pinch of SALT

PEPPER to taste

1 48-ounce (1.4-*l*) can V-8 JUICE

28 ounces (795 ml) WATER

6 14-ounce (398-ml) tins COCONUT MILK

7 cups (1.75 *l*) BUTTERNUT SQUASH, peeled, cut into 1-inch (2.5-cm) cubes

5 cups (1.25 *l*) SPINACH, coarsely chopped

juice of 3 to 4 LIMES, or to taste

In a large soup pot: Heat the olive or canola oil and sauté the onions and garlic a few minutes. Add the ginger, salt, and pepper and continue to sauté until the onions are softened. Add the v-8 juice and the spice mixture and simmer for about 5 minutes, stirring to coat the vegetables with the spices. Stir in the coconut milk and add the squash. Gently simmer uncovered for about 40 minutes, or until the squash is tender. Taste for seasoning, add more spices if desired. Cool. Refrigerate.

Just before serving, chop the spinach and add to the soup along with the lime juice to taste. Add a little more v-8 juice and water if it seems too thick. Best made a day ahead.

New Mexico Corn Chowder

I had fun playing around with the tastes of New Mexico to come up with this new soup to open the Tomato. Great for entertaining on a ski weekend. Like most of our soups, it's a meal in itself. For those who go for the really hot stuff, add more chili powder and Tabasco, or fresh chili peppers. Serves 12 to 16.

3 tablespoons (45 ml) OLIVE or CANOLA OIL

1 red, 1 yellow, 1 green PEPPER, julienned

3 ONIONS, in small slices

4 to 5 cloves GARLIC, finely chopped

2 6 ½-ounce (185-ml) cans green CHILIES, chopped

8 cups (2 *l*) V-8 JUICE

8 cups (2 *l*) TOMATO JUICE

5 10-ounce (284-ml) cans CAMPBELL'S TOMATO SOUP

2 28-ounce (795-ml) cans PLUM TOMATOES, coarsely chopped

5 cups (1250 ml) frozen CORN NIBLETS, or mixture of frozen and canned

3 to 4 tablespoons (45 to 60 ml) ground CUMIN

3 to 4 tablespoons (45 to 60 ml) CHILI POWDER

One of our customers exclaimed one day, "This soup is unusually hot today! What have you added to it? Could I have more water, please?" As she continued to cough, I went and tasted it myself and realized that a chef had added cayenne powder instead of sweet paprika! Later, when the guilty chef came on duty, I told him to close his eyes and put out his tongue. Then I said, "Here's a little taste test," and put some cayenne on his tongue. He coughed a bit and ran for water. Then I did the same with sweet paprika. Now he'll never forget to taste everything he makes. I know I never have. I can still feel the heat from the time one of the chefs I worked with exploded my taste buds in a similar fashion.

SALT and PEPPER to taste

several shots of TABASCO, to taste

2 tablespoons (30 ml) WORCESTERSHIRE SAUCE

Toppings for soup:

TORTILLA CHIPS, coarsely broken

MONTEREY JACK CHEESE, grated

In a large stockpot, heat the oil and sauté the peppers, onion, and garlic until softened and caramelized, about 10 to 15 minutes. Add the rest of the ingredients and simmer about 30 minutes to 1 hour. Add more v-8 juice and tomato juice if it seems too thick. Best made a day ahead.

To serve: Pour into soup bowls, sprinkle with a little tortillas and cheese on top.

Gazpacho

Once June rolls around we start to serve this traditional cold Spanish soup. My version is extra chunky and not too hot, so you can taste the marvellous fresh flavour of vegetables. Make it days in advance, as this soup improves with age. Serves 8 to 10.

4 very ripe large TOMATOES

1 14-ounce (398 ml) can TOMATOES

½ ONION

2 ENGLISH CUCUMBERS, unpeeled

2 RED PEPPERS, seeded

4 sprigs PARSLEY

2 cloves GARLIC, crushed

10 ounces (284 ml) V-8 JUICE

2 cups (500 ml) TOMATO JUICE

juice of ½ LEMON

½ cup (125 ml) HEINZ CHILI SAUCE

3 tablespoons (45 ml) fresh BASIL,
or ½ teaspoon (2.5 ml) dry

Okayama City, Japan, is home to the head office of the Tomato Bank. Their mascot – a giant tomato – is called Tokkun. The staff at the Tomato Bank wear buttons and pins on their uniforms with the bank logo – the tomato – and start each day with their very own Tomato Song. Why a tomato bank? Apparently the tomato represents power and the bank owners felt that the name would appeal to a new generation of customers. Every customer who opens an account with the bank receives a book containing pictures of, and short essays and poems about, tomatoes.

3 tablespoons (45 ml) fresh DILL,
or ½ teaspoon (2.5 ml) dry

½ teaspoon (2.5 ml) dried OREGANO

½ teaspoon (2.5 ml) Hungarian or Spanish SWEET PAPRIKA

1 tablespoon (15 ml) WHITE WINE VINEGAR

½ teaspoon (2.5 ml) WORCESTERSHIRE SAUCE

Toppings for soup:

CROUTONS

chopped GREEN ONIONS

Naturally, we had to have a tomato soup on the menu. When we first devised the menu, Jennifer said, "Mom, it would be fun to include the diner classic, Campbell's tomato soup, made with milk and topped with saltines." We thought very few would order it. How wrong we were! Seems we all remember the comfort of that creamy tomato soup with saltine crackers crumbled on top. You'd be surprised how many cans we go through in a week.

At least 3 days before serving, cut the tomatoes, onion, cucumber, and peppers into chunks. Put them through a food processor with the parsley, garlic, v-8 juice, and tomato juice, processing a portion at a time, with an on/off motion. Add the rest of the ingredients and blend slightly. Do not overprocess, keep the mixture chunky. If you prefer a thinner soup, add more tomato juice and experiment with the herbs and seasonings until the soup is to your liking. Cover and refrigerate. Will keep for 4 to 5 days.

Serve in small bowls and pass the croutons and onions.

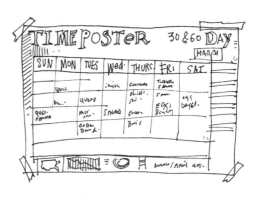

Chef Glenys Morgan's Soup Creations

We call Glenys Morgan a saint at the Tomato. She is not only our food consultant and jack-of-all-trades, she is the best soup maker in the world. Her sense of flavour and balance are superb. These are some of her masterpieces that her faithful soup fans have been waiting for.

Two *Tomato* Basil Onion

The Two Tomato Basil Onion soup boasts the best canned tomatoes you can find, with sun-dried tomatoes added for that extra dimension. For a spicier rendition, known as the Italian Arrabiata soup, add a little dried red pepper flakes to taste. Serves 10 to 12 generously.

¼ cup (60 ml) OLIVE or CANOLA OIL

3 to 4 cloves GARLIC, finely chopped (optional)

4 large ONIONS, sliced in thin slivers

1 ½ cups (375 ml) SUN-DRIED TOMATOES, chopped

PEPPER to taste

2 100-ounce (2.8-*l*) cans CRUSHED TOMATOES

1 48-ounce (1.4-*l*) can TOMATO JUICE

¼ cup (60 ml) dry BASIL

3 bunches fresh BASIL, leaves removed
from stems and julienned

½ cup (125 ml) PESTO, for finishing the soup

In a large stockpot, heat the oil and sauté the garlic (optional) and the onions until they are softened and slightly caramelized. Add the crushed tomatoes. Add the tomato juice to give the soup the desired semi-thick consistency. Add water to thin it out if necessary.

Add the sun-dried tomatoes, pepper, but *no salt*. Since the sun-dried tomatoes are salted during the drying process there will be enough to flavour the soup. Add the dry basil and bring to a boil. Taste and add the fresh julienned basil. Before serving, swirl in the pesto for extra basil.

Whenever Allan Morgan made his famous borscht, the children in the restaurant would come into the kitchen and see Big Al's large purple hands after he peeled all those beets. We told the kids that he was our "Martian chef." Being an actor, Al would then rush off to do a play reading, all the time keeping his hands in his pockets. Finally, one morning, he came on duty wearing surgical gloves to perform his borscht operation. Nowadays we order peeled beets. You live and learn.

Santa Fe Corn *Chowder*
with Cinnamon, Basil, and Chilies

This soup is amazing. Your taste buds will pop trying to decipher what exactly the ingredients are! We keep our customers guessing. Now you know the secret. Serves 8 to 10.

We have served over a quarter of a million tomatoes at the Tomato.

4 cups (1 *l*) MILK or LIGHT CREAM, or a combination of both

12 each CORIANDER SEEDS, PEPPERCORNS, and CLOVES

1 CINNAMON STICK

small bunch of BASIL LEAVES

few sprigs CILANTRO and MINT (if available)

5 to 6 ears of CORN, or 4 cups (1 *l*) CORN KERNELS

2 medium ONIONS, diced

inner leaves of CELERY, finely minced

2 to 3 JALAPENOS, or roasted POBLANO CHILI, minced

3 tablespoons (45 ml) BUTTER or OIL

4 cups (1 *l*) MILK, STOCK, or WATER for finishing the soup

Place the milk, spices, and herbs in a saucepan and slowly bring to the scalding point. Let the infusion steep while preparing the other vegetables, or prepare ahead. The longer it steeps, the more flavourful the broth. Heat the butter in a stockpot, add the onion and celery, and sauté until softened. For a richer flavour, brown the onion but watch carefully not to burn. The soup will have a more pronounced onion flavour. Add the second litre of milk (or the liquid) and bring to the scalding point. This will lift the sautéed celery off the bottom of the pot. Simmer for a few minutes. Strain the infusion of herbs and spices from the milk and add to the stockpot with the corn. Simmer to reduce slightly, then add the minced chilies, salt, to taste, and minced coriander if desired.

Note: This soup is best made when the corn is in season and sweet, but during the winter frozen corn makes a nice substitute. If the corn seems a little tough or starchy, a combination of frozen niblets and canned niblets gives a sweeter flavour. If the soup seems thinner than desired, purée some canned niblets and add to the milk broth.

Sweet Potato Soup

This is a creamy puréed soup without the calories! Rich in flavour, it's the perfect soup for the autumn and winter months. Try a swirl of yogurt on top of each serving with chopped cilantro. I prefer using yams, instead of sweet potatoes, for more intense flavour and colour. Serves 6 to 8.

2 tablespoons (30 ml) BUTTER

2 medium ONIONS, chopped

1 clove GARLIC, minced

¼ cup (60 ml) dry WHITE WINE

1 pound (500 g) YAMS or SWEET POTATOES, peeled and diced

1 medium JALAPENO, seeded and chopped

4 cups (1 *l*) CHICKEN STOCK

¼ teaspoon (1 ml) each dry THYME,
TARRAGON, and ROSEMARY

¼ teaspoon (1 ml) NUTMEG

SALT and PEPPER

¼ cup (60 ml) chopped CHIVES, parsley, or cilantro

In a stockpot, melt the butter and sauté the onions and garlic over medium heat until softened. Slightly brown the onions, don't burn. Add the wine, potatoes, and jalapenos. Cook covered for about 15 minutes, or until the potatoes are slightly soft. Add the stock, dry herbs, and nutmeg. Bring to a boil, cover, and simmer for about 15 minutes more. Add salt and pepper to taste. Purée in a food processor until smooth. If the soup is thicker than desired, add a little more of the chicken stock. When ready to serve, reheat and garnish with sprigs of chosen fresh herbs.

Whisky Smoked Salmon Chowder

Growing up in the Maritimes meant that we always had an abundance of seafood chowders at home. From clams, salmon, halibut, cod, scallops, to lobster, you name it, we had it! I never imagined I would find seafood any better.

When we opened the Tomato, we tried a lot of excellent smoked salmon, until one stood out above all the others, the Westcoast Select Indian candy salmon is superior. Put out by Sundance Seafood Company in Vancouver, it is out of this world. One hundred percent B.C. wild salmon with no additives, premium quality. Glenys takes this "smoked to perfection salmon" and makes a chowder equal to any I have ever tasted. It is the star blue plate special whenever we feature it. It's a total meal in itself, along with hearty grain breads. Serves 10 to 12.

¼ cup (60 ml) BUTTER

2 ONIONS, chopped, then minced in
food processor, very fine

5 sticks CELERY, chopped, then minced in
food processor, very fine

16 small raw red or white POTATOES, diced into 4 to 5 pieces

5 sticks CELERY, thinly sliced on the diagonal

SALT and PEPPER

2 cups (500 ml) WHOLE MILK, or more

2 cups (500 ml) WATER, or more

2 ½ cups (625 ml) CORN

1 cup (250 ml) CREAMO

1 cup (250 ml) CREAM

1 ½ pounds (750 g) WESTCOAST SELECT SALMON,
skinned, sliced into small pieces (any Indian candy
smoked salmon can be substituted)

1 bunch fresh DILL

2 ounces (30 ml) JACK DANIEL'S BOURBON

The *Vancouver Sun*'s food critic, Karen Krangle, wrote this about our tomato soup: "If there ever was a North American comfort food, it would have to be canned cream of tomato soup (yes, that brand), made with milk and served with crackers that you can crumble up and mush into it. It's the kind of thing you remember coming home to at lunch time on crisp November schooldays, or maybe drowning your teenage sorrows in on a dull Friday night. It's not, however, the sort of thing you'd expect to see on a restaurant menu. But at the Tomato, the

In a stockpot, melt the butter and sauté the minced onions and celery until softened. Add the potatoes and sliced celery, mixing well. Add the milk and water, adding more if necessary, just to cover the vegetables. Add a little salt and pepper. The Westcoast Select salmon is peppered, so add accordingly. Cook until the potatoes are soft, about 30 minutes. Add the rest of the ingredients. *Do not boil*, as the milk will curdle. Keep on low. Add more creamo to thin it out, as it will thicken as it simmers.

cheery little café, there it is, billed as a 'diner classic.' So, whenever they are adding the final touches to their hearty borscht or a spicy New Mexico Corn Chowder and an order comes in for 'a Campbell's,' they shout, 'How can they do this to us? It's an insult!' as they reluctantly zap a bowl in the microwave." We put Campbell's Tomato on the menu almost as a joke, but if we took it off now, we would have many unhappy customers. I must admit that once in a while I, too, crave that comfort soup of the fifties.

The Sandwich Board

THE TOMATO is known for its homestyle, gutsy sandwiches. When we opened we wanted to feature sandwiches with a difference – the best bread we could find, fresh roasted turkey, our own cranberry relish and special mayonnaise spreads, B.C. smoked salmon, and the finest of cheeses, including Danish fontina, chèvre, aged cheddar, and Danish Gouda.

Our customers tell us we have the greatest *mucho grande* sandwiches anywhere! We like to think the customer is always right!

The Tomato Cold
Sandwiches

Served on either hand-cut or sourdough bread, these are a few of our feature sandwiches:

Tomato's Tomato

Pesto Mayonnaise (see Give Me the Works! for recipe), tomatoes, red onions, and butter or leafy lettuce (depending on season and prices).

From the Garden

Roasted Pepper Mayonnaise (see Give Me the Works! for recipe), tomatoes, cucumbers, cream cheese, and butter or leafy lettuce (depending on season and prices).

B.C. Smoked Salmon on a Bagel

A West Coast tradition. Cream cheese, capers, and red onions.

French Afternoon or Evening

Very romantic, very popular. Take a wedge of Brie, fresh seasonal fruit, toasted sourdough bread, add a crisp Chardonnay. Ooh la la!

Peanut Butter and Banana

For the kid in all of us! Add gooey jam if you like!

The Gooda Sandwich

Smoked Gouda cheese, cucumbers, mayonnaise, and butter or leafy lettuce (depending on season and prices), on sun-dried tomato bread. A unique combo!

Did you know that 1 pound (500 g) of tomatoes equals 2 large, 3 medium, or 4 small tomatoes; 14 to 20 cherry tomatoes; or 1 cup (250 ml) of coarsely chopped tomatoes?

Roast Chicken
with Lime or Lemon Basil Mayonnaise

A blue plate feature from time to time – an automatic sellout. Makes 4 sandwiches.

8 slices MULTIGRAIN or SOURDOUGH BREAD, or try BAGUETTES, split in half

2 cups (500 ml) cooked CHICKEN BREASTS, cut into ½-inch (12-mm) cubes

3 CELERY sticks, finely chopped

PEPPER to taste

juice of 2 LEMONS or LIMES

½ cup (125 ml) MAYONNAISE

2 teaspoons (5 ml) DIJON MUSTARD

⅓ cup (80 ml) fresh BASIL, chopped

butter or leafy LETTUCE (depending on season and prices)

½ an ENGLISH CUCUMBER, unpeeled, thinly sliced, pat dry

extra MAYONNAISE

Jurgen Gothe, one of Canada's premier food critics and a columnist for the *Vancouver Sun*, had this to say about the Tomato's sandwiches: "The take-out division of the Tomato Café is also home of the famous Tomato's Tomato (quintessence of fresh tomato with pesto and purple onion). But this one is made with big, fat, dense, white, country farm-style bread with a good crust on – slabs of it, all irregular and hand-cut. Open wide and say ahhh! You will, too, once you hit those slabs of fresh-roasted turkey breast, plus cranberry chutney, lettuce, mayo. Don't ask for extra salt. It really doesn't need it – maybe a tad more pepper, that's it. A tasty, roasty, homey sandwich, the kind Lawrence Sanders's Detective Delaney would eat standing over the kitchen sink. Actually, if you're careful and keep the paper bag in the same hand as you're eating with, you'll do only minimal damage to your shirt. Two splodges!"

Combine all except the extra mayonnaise and cucumbers. Add more lemon or lime juice for a tarter taste.

To serve: Spread a little mayonnaise on the bread, top with a few leaves of lettuce on one side. Divide the chicken salad on top of the lettuce for 4 sandwiches (allow ½ cup [125 ml] chicken salad per sandwich). Top with a thin layer of cucumbers, then with the bread. Cut in half on the diagonal and serve.

Note: You may wish to leave the cucumbers for a side garnish with a strip of red pepper.

Hot Off *the* Grill:
The Tomato Hot Sandwiches

There is something comforting and decadent at the same time, as we take the first bite of cheese oozing out of a fabulous thick grilled sandwich. I would say it's rather sensuous! Our customers must agree, as our chefs are constantly on the run, trying to keep up with our grilled sandwich orders. We offer six grilled sandwich items on our menu and, from time to time, blue plate specials. At the Tomato, we serve our grilled sandwiches with a side of our Creamy Potato Dill Salad (see Salad Time for recipe), or seasonal greens with a choice of our Basil Vinaigrette, Orange Mustard Ginger, or Yogurt Dill dressings (see Give Me the Works! for these and other dressing recipes).

Our menu features the classic diner BLT, with lean bacon, lettuce, tomato, and Roasted Pepper Mayonnaise (see Give Me the Works! for recipe). We also serve a Tomato Club with roasted turkey breast, lean bacon, aged cheddar, tomatoes, of course, and Roasted Pepper Mayonnaise. As we say on the menu, "Join it! It's huge!" And for the cheese lovers, we have the Double Double with aged cheddar, Danish fontina, and roasted peppers. Add lean bacon for the absolute ultimate sandwich affair.

My choice is our TCOP – a nickname for our tomato, cheese, onion, and pesto sandwich. We describe it as "tomatoes, fontina cheese, onion, and pesto, open and facing you," waiting to be devoured.

Our all-time bestselling item is the old-fashioned turkey sandwich on sourdough bread with my special cranberry relish. We've sold thousands and thousands of them. We've also sold a few sans turkey. This is especially unfortunate when it is a take-out order and the justifiably angry, hungry, and turkeyless customer is yelling at you over his car phone while stuck in a three-hour lineup waiting to board the ferry to Vancouver Island.

For one serving:

1 ½ ½-inch (12-mm) slices of SOURDOUGH BREAD

⅓ cup (80 ml) Danish FONTINA CHEESE, grated

about 4 tablespoons (60 ml) PESTO MAYONNAISE
(see Give Me the Works! for recipe)

1 ½ pieces of SUN-DRIED TOMATO, softened

6 ¼-inch (6-mm) slices of TOMATO

a few paper-thin slices of RED ONION

Did you know that tomatoes, along with potatoes and lettuce, are the top-grossing vegetables in North America?

To SERVE: Grill the bread until golden. Place on a cookie sheet. On each piece of bread, spread a layer of the Pesto Mayonnaise, saving some for the topping. Divide the cheese evenly over each of the three pieces of bread. Add more if you like. Grill until the cheese is melted. Top each piece with 2 slices of tomato, a little pesto, and a slice of the sun-dried tomato. Add a sprinkle of the onions over each piece and serve immediately.

NOTE: If you wish, you can pop the tomatoes under the grill to heat slightly before adding the Pesto Mayonnaise and sun-dried tomatoes.

Grilled Chicken *Sandwich*

Our Roasted Pepper Mayonnaise makes this sandwich unique. For one serving:

2 ½-inch (12-mm) slices SOURDOUGH

1 CHICKEN BREAST, grilled

1 small can ROASTED PEPPERS

about 4 tablespoons (60 ml) ROASTED PEPPER
MAYONNAISE (see Give Me the Works! for recipe)

To SERVE: Grill the bread until golden. On each piece of bread, spread a layer of the Roasted Pepper Mayonnaise.

On 1 piece of the bread, top the mayonnaise spread with a layer of sliced roasted peppers. Top with 1 grilled chicken breast, sliced. Put the other piece of bread on top and slice in half. Serve immediately.

Open-faced
Focaccia

When Ecco Il Pane – a Vancouver speciality bread company – opened, they made our first Tomato bread, with roasted tomatoes, cumin, and garlic highlighting the flavours. We then began to experiment with grilled sandwiches to complement these marvellous tastes. Then along came their black olive bread and the Italian favourite, focaccia. Try these for a new sandwich adventure!

Serve with tossed greens and your favourite dressing.

FOCACCIA BREAD, sliced in wedges or squares (you can substitute sourdough, French, or a heavy grain bread)

JAPANESE EGGPLANT, thinly sliced and grilled

ROASTED RED PEPPERS, sliced in strips and grilled

fresh BASIL, shredded into thin strips

DANISH FONTINA, CHÈVRE, or MONTEREY JACK, shredded

ROASTED PEPPER MAYONNAISE (see Give Me the Works! for recipe)

To SERVE: Grill the focaccia bread. Spread with about 1 to 2 tablespoons (15 to 30 ml) Roasted Pepper Mayonnaise. Top with a layer of the Japanese eggplant, roasted peppers, and cheese. Place under the grill until the cheese is melted. Top with a few strips of fresh basil.

NOTE: At the Tomato we sometimes include thinly sliced grilled zucchini or mushrooms for a power-packed sandwich.

Angela Murrills, the food critic for *The Georgia Straight*, caught the nature of the Tomato's sandwiches just right: "All of the Tomato's sandwiches are two-fisters – hefty doorsteps of multigrain, sourdough, or flax bread wrapped around tomato, red onion, and pesto mayonnaise, or cheddar and fontina cheeses and roasted peppers. They're sandwiches large enough to share. Leftover bread shows up as croutons in a particularly zingy Caesar salad. Flavours are bold and clear, and whoever assembles the plates has a healthy free spirit."

Salad Time

ICEBERG LETTUCE, leafy greens, and romaine were the extent of greens available a decade ago. The classic Caesar has been around since the early fifties as the ultimate in salads. Now we have every conceivable salad green imaginable, with 6 to 8 gourmet greens as a daily feature in most restaurants and markets.

At the Tomato, we serve organic greens with our own dressings and, of course, the Caesar reigns supreme! For the undecided, we offer our Salad Trio, a sampling of 3 different salads – "a salad buffet" – with bread. Perfect for the undecided.

Tomato's
Caesar

Sharon Woyat first introduced me to her Caesar salad dressing many, many years ago. It was my family's favourite, and now my Tomato family of customers keep coming back for more. Serves 8.

2 large EGGS

6 tablespoons (90 ml) LEMON JUICE

PEPPER to taste

1 large clove GARLIC, crushed

½ cup (125 ml) finely grated PARMESAN CHEESE

1 small can ANCHOVIES, including oil

½ cup (125 ml) OLIVE OIL, or a blend of olive and salad oil

fresh grated PARMESAN CHEESE for topping

CROUTONS

ROMAINE LETTUCE

"Tomato arguably has the best Caesar salad in Vancouver, and some even say Canada!"
— *Terminal City*,
September 14, 1994

In a food processor, blend everything but the olive oil, then pour the oil slowly to thicken.

At the Tomato, we serve the Caesar with enough dressing to coat, topped with a sprinkle of croutons and Parmesan cheese.

The Tomato Croutons

Commercial croutons cannot compare with the crispiness and flavour of homemade ones. At the Tomato, we mix our multigrain and sourdough breads to make our delicious croutons.

4 to 6 cups (1 to 1.5 *l*) small BREAD CUBES

4 to 6 large cloves GARLIC, crushed (optional)

1 cup (250 ml) PARMESAN CHEESE

about ½ cup (125 ml) OLIVE OIL,
or a blend of olive and salad oils

Set the oven at 300° F (150° C). In a large bowl, toss the bread cubes with the garlic and Parmesan cheese. Drizzle enough of the oil over top, just to coat the cubes, and toss. Bake for about 40 to 45 minutes, stirring the cubes after 20 minutes, until they are golden, crisp, and dry. Taste a few, they should be crunchy. Cool, store in the fridge for weeks.

NOTE: My pet peeve is having limp romaine. Make sure you pat your lettuce dry, layer with paper towels in between in a plastic container. Should keep several days in the fridge, if prepped properly.

One of our customers heaped extravagant praise on our Caesar salad as he devoured it. Then he asked the waiter for a Caesar to go and said, "Put a rush on it, please. I'm on my way to the airport to catch a flight to Toronto. It'll be my dinner."

John's Tex-Mex *Black Bean* and *Corn* Salad

John McKinstry, one of our original Master Chefs, came up with his speciality salad to complement our Santa Fe Corn Pie (see The Tomato Classics for recipe). John is an avid gardener and antique collector, and is active in the theatre community. To top it off, John is a real Fred Astaire when it comes to square dancing!

John and Allan Morgan have become true lifetime friends and both represent the real spirit of what a professional chef should be.

This colourful salad is perfect with summer barbecue buffet favourites. Serves 10 to 12 as a side dish.

1 to 1 ½ (250 to 375 ml) dried BLACK BEANS

Put into a large pot of boiling water and cover. Simmer about 1 hour, or until tender. Drain, rinse well in cold water. For quicker cooking, soak overnight in water and cover. Toss with the following:

2 cups (500 ml) frozen CORN NIBLETS, thawed, or canned

1 red and 1 yellow PEPPER, diced

3 JALAPENOS, seeded and diced

¾ cup (180 ml) RED ONIONS, chopped

½ cup (125 ml) CILANTRO, chopped

Now toss with the dressing:

½ cup (125 ml) SALAD or OLIVE OIL

3 tablespoons (45 ml) red wine VINEGAR, or to taste

juice of 3 LIMES

2 teaspoons (10 ml) CUMIN, or to taste

1 teaspoon (5 ml) CHILI POWDER, or to taste

1 teaspoon (5 ml) SUGAR

1 large clove GARLIC, crushed

PEPPER to taste

pinch of SALT

Blend well. Best made the day ahead. Refrigerate, will keep for several days.

Salade Niçoise

In the summer at the Tomato we feature blue plate salads that are a meal in themselves. This French classic is one of my all-time favourites, and my customers agree because we're always selling out! Serves 6 as a main course.

1 ½ pounds (750 g) fresh GREEN BEANS, blanched, cut in half

1 pound (500 g) cooked small red or white
POTATOES, cut in half

1 6 ½-ounce (184-g) tin solid white TUNA,
drained, cut into chunks

1 large ENGLISH CUCUMBER, unpeeled, cut into
chunks, pat dry

½ cup (125 ml) CALAMATA OLIVES

PEPPER to taste

pinch of SALT

2 medium TOMATOES, or 5 ROMA TOMATOES,
cut into quarters

butter or romaine LETTUCE

At the Tomato, we mix all the ingredients in a large bowl, then toss with enough dressing to coat well. You can also layer the ingredients in an attractive glass bowl, topping with additional tomatoes, cucumbers, and olives. Drained slices of anchovies can be added on top as well.

Several hours before serving: In a large bowl, gently toss all the ingredients, except the tomatoes and lettuce. Add enough of the dressing to coat everything well. Add a little extra because the potatoes will absorb a lot of the dressing. Refrigerate for several hours for the flavours to blend.

TO SERVE: Line a large salad platter or individual salad plates with the lettuce, then add the salad on top and decorate with the tomato wedges and a sprig of fresh dill. Serve with lots of hearty grain or French bread. Add more tuna if desired.

French Dressing for Salade Niçoise

This dressing goes well with any greens. You should have extra to store in the fridge for another time.

1 ½ cups (375 ml) OLIVE OIL

1 ½ cups (375 ml) SALAD OIL

⅓ cup (75 ml) WHITE WINE VINEGAR

2 cloves GARLIC, pressed

1 teaspoon (5 ml) DIJON MUSTARD

1 teaspoon (5 ml) WHITE SUGAR

juice of 2 LEMONS

3 tablespoons (45 ml) GREEN ONIONS or CHIVES, chopped

2 tablespoons (30 ml) SHALLOTS, chopped (optional)

1 teaspoon (5 ml) dried OREGANO

¼ cup (60 ml) fresh BASIL, chopped,
or 1 teaspoon (5 ml) dried

"Hi, my name is Jack Henry. I'm a baby. I was born on August 23, 1994, which isn't such a big deal unless you know the rest of my story. You see, I wasn't due to be born until November 15. On August 19 my mom was paddling with her Dragon Boat team for the opening of the Commonwealth Games in Victoria. She was 6 ½ months pregnant and suddenly didn't feel very well, so she left her team in Victoria and came back to Vancouver early. You guessed it! I was the reason she didn't feel well. I wanted out. And at 3:24 a.m. on August 23 out I came, just under 3 pounds, and not breathing very well. I spent about a week on a ventilator in an incubator, with many bells and whistles

¼ cup (60 ml) fresh DILL, chopped,
or 1 teaspoon (5 ml) dried

¼ cup (60 ml) fresh PARSLEY, chopped,
or 1 teaspoon (5 ml) dried

Several days before using: Whisk the ingredients to blend well. Store in the fridge. For a tarter dressing, add more lemon juice or vinegar.

NOTE: The Tomato's Basil Vinaigrette (See Give Me the Works! for recipe) is a perfect alternative to the French dressing. Try it as well sometime.

Moroccan Vegetable *Salad*

I call this my "power salad." Chock-full of everything good for you, a scrumptious salad with its Middle Eastern spices and its crunchy textures. Serves 10 to 12.

4 cups (1 *l*) small MUSHROOMS, halved

4 cups (1 *l*) CHERRY TOMATOES

1 19-ounce (540-ml) can GARBANZO BEANS
or CHICK PEAS, drained

1 cup (250 ml) large BLACK OLIVES, halved, or whole
Calamata olives

2 cups (500 ml) CELERY, sliced on the diagonal

1 each red, yellow, orange PEPPERS, thinly sliced

1 cup (250 ml) RED ONIONS, finely chopped

3 JALAPENOS, seeded, finely chopped

⅓ cup (80 ml) fresh CILANTRO, chopped

LETTUCE GREENS

Dressing:

¾ cup (180 ml) PLAIN YOGURT

¾ cup (180 ml) MAYONNAISE

attached. At 4 pounds they let me sleep in a cot, and at 6 ½ pounds they sent me home. During my stay in the hospital, my parents spent a lot of time there comforting me. Just down the road from the hospital is a great little café called the Tomato. My parents spent a lot of time there, too, eating TCOPs and drinking chocolate shakes. My dad and mom told the staff all about me, so when I got out of the hospital, they took me to the Tomato to meet everybody. I liked it there so much that my parents keep taking me back. In fact, I've been there so much that the staff made me Customer of the Month. What an honour! I can't wait till I can eat there, too!"

2 tablespoons (30 ml) OLIVE OIL

juice of 1 LEMON

2 cloves GARLIC, crushed

PEPPER to taste

2 teaspoons (10 ml) CUMIN

2 teaspoons (10 ml) TURMERIC

1 teaspoon (5 ml) mild CURRY POWDER

¼ cup (60 ml) fresh DILL, chopped,
or 1 ½ teaspoons (7 ml) dried

Is it the attack of the killer tomatoes? Each year revellers hurl
tons of soggy tomatoes at one
another in a small Spanish town
called Brenol during what's
known as the Tomato Festival.
It draws over 25,000 tomato
fans annually, flinging and eating tomatoes with great abandon. Not a festival to wear
white, of course!

Days ahead: Combine the dressing ingredients and refrigerate.

The day ahead or morning of serving (best made a day
ahead): In a large salad bowl, toss all the vegetables, except
the lettuce. Add enough dressing to coat well. Cover and
refrigerate. Serve on a bed of greens. Pass more dressing if
there is any left over. Great served with grilled or warmed
pita bread.

Tomato Basil
Onion Salad

Doug's all-time favourite salad is the Tomato Basil Onion,
and judging from the number of orders we serve at the
Tomato, I would say our customers feel the same way.

Line each salad plate with 3 to 4 BUTTER LETTUCE leaves.
Slice 2 medium TOMATOES and 2 ROMA TOMATOES into ¼-
inch (6-mm) slices. Arrange artistically on top of the lettuce
leaves. Top with a few thin slices of RED ONION. Sprinkle
with about 6 to 8 roasted PINE NUTS. Drizzle about 3 to 4
tablespoons (45 to 60 ml) BASIL VINAIGRETTE (see Give Me
the Works! for recipe) over the tomatoes.

Note: 4 to 5 small halves of fresh bocconcini can be added.

Creamy
Potato Dill Salad

"Like no other," our menu states and, for me, I just had to serve the potato salad my family grew up on. I think it is one of our ultimate comfort foods at the Tomato. Everyone can relate to their childhood and summer picnics with Mom's own special potato salad.

We serve it with our grilled sandwiches and as a side salad. Everyone asks, "What exactly do you put in the salad?" My response, "It's the addition of grainy Dijon mustard and a little sour cream that makes the difference." "Ahhh, that's what it is!" Serves 8 to 12.

8 cups (2 *l*) cooked baby NEW POTATOES, red or white

about 1 cup (250 ml) small PURPLE ONIONS,
finely chopped

2 cups (500 ml) MAYONNAISE

½ cup (125 ml) SOUR CREAM

⅓ cup (80 ml) grainy DIJON MUSTARD

lots of freshly cracked PEPPER

½ cup (125 ml) fresh DILL, chopped

Cut the potatoes into halves or quarters. Add the rest of the ingredients to make a super creamy combination. Can be made a day ahead. Add more pepper or grainy Dijon mustard if desired.

Les Dames Pacific Northwest Salad

Serves 6.

Les Dames d'Escoffier is a networking group of women in the food and wine related fields. This year we held a fundraiser with three cooking classes to establish a scholarship fund for women aspiring to further their knowledge in these fields. The Delta Place Spring Culinary Celebration, held in the elegant Crystal Room at the Delta Place Hotel in Vancouver, was sold out.

Five of Vancouver's Les Dames' chefs presented their signature dishes. We were fortunate to bring in Monique Barbeau, born in Vancouver, now the reigning chef of the four-star restaurant, Fullers, in Seattle, Washington, for our closing class.

As one of the five chefs, along with cookbook authors Caren McSherry Valagao and Kasey Wilson, Lesley Stowe, owner, Lesley Stowe Fine Foods, Margaret Chisholm, director of cooking classes, Dubrulle French Culinary School, I chose the salad course.

This salad reflects the flavours of our Northwest and is one of the most popular dishes at the Tomato. We use the famous Westcoast Select Indian candy smoked salmon from British Columbia for our presentation. It is the best in the world.

Because of the seasonal nature of wild mushrooms, at the Tomato we substitute a few julienne strips of red and yellow peppers. These can be added as a garnish, without sautéing them.

½ pound (250 g) INDIAN CANDY SMOKED SALMON (such as Westcoast Select)

3 cups (750 ml) mixed WILD MUSHROOMS (e.g. shiitake, oyster, chanterelle)

2 tablespoons (30 ml) OLIVE OIL

2 tablespoons (30 ml) BUTTER

Since we opened our doors at the Tomato, artists, actors, musicians, and writers have found a home either as staff, customers, or performers. Here are a just a few of them. Juno award winner Ian Tamblyn gave 2 benefit concerts for Green Thumb Theatre. Canadian actress Claire Coulter performed Wallace Shawn's *The Fever* as a benefit for Pink Ink Theatre. Over 25 local artists have had their work displayed on the café's walls. In conjunction with the New Play Centre and the Betty Lambert Society, the Tomato has hosted a series of playwrights' cabarets where such celebrated dramatists as Tom Cone, Joan Macleod, Morris Panych, David King,

freshly ground PEPPER to taste

1 pound (500 g) mixed seasonal FIELD GREENS

8 ounces (225 g) CHEVRE or goat's cheese, crumbled

MAPLE BALSAMIC VINAIGRETTE
(see Give Me the Works! for recipe)

Peel the skin off the salmon, slice in finger-length strips, and set aside. Remove the stems from the mushrooms and slice the caps thinly. Just before serving, heat the oil and butter in a skillet, add the mushrooms and sauté until softened. Add pepper to taste and keep warm.

Divide the greens evenly among 6 salad plates, mounding them high. Sprinkle about 2 tablespoons (30 ml) of chèvre over the greens. Stand the salmon strips upright against the greens, arranging them around the mound. Divide mushrooms evenly around the outside of each plate. Drizzle a little of the warm Maple Balsamic Vinaigrette over the greens and serve immediately. Pass more dressing, if desired.

NOTE: At the Tomato, we heat up the Maple Balsamic Vinaigrette in a sautéing pan, add the salmon pieces, and simmer a few minutes until warm.

Colin Thomas, John Lazarus, Dennis Foon, and Sally Clarke have read from their work. Terry David Mulligan has shot *MuchWest* at the restaurant, and we've also had a Zeller's ad, several student films, and some episodes of the television shows *Robin's Hoods* and *Madison* done here. Other celebrities to frequent the Tomato are singer Sarah McLachlan, the writer and director of *My American Cousin*, Sandy Wilson, Blue Rodeo singers Greg Keelor and Jim Cuddy, and Bryan Adams's manager, Bruce Allen. Oh, yes, and Weird Al Yankovic was once interviewed at the Tomato.

Give Me the Works!

Condiments

At the Tomato, we don't make our mayonnaises from scratch, but we give a special personality to our sandwich spreads by adding little Tomato "teasers."

We found that the commercial Hellmann's or Kraft's Real mayonnaise work well as a base for our spreads.

I thought I was crazy about tomatoes until I met 3 wild tomato fanatics, Terry Van Roon, Scott Olson, and Chris Kielesinski. With hundreds of facts and tales about tomatoes from around the world, they're the number one tomato trivia experts. Each year they host their Tomato Love-in – a dinner featuring a tomato dish for every course. Would you believe one of them even painted a giant tomato on his car?

Chipotle* Mayonnaise

Makes 1 cup (250 ml).

1 cup (250 ml) MAYONNAISE
1 to 2 canned smoked whole CHIPOTLES, chopped, to taste

Combine in a food processor until smooth. Add more or less chipotles depending on how hot you want the mayonnaise. Refrigerate, will keep for several days.

* CHIPOTLE: When the chili jalapeno is dried and smoked, it becomes the chili chipotle, dark brown in colour, smoky in flavour, and hot to taste. A little goes a long way. The canned chipotles are available at most Mexican specialty counters.

Sour Cream Chipotle Sauce

Great with all Mexican dishes.

1 cup (250 ml) SOUR CREAM
1 to 2 canned smoked whole CHIPOTLES, chopped

Follow the same method as with the Chipotle Mayonnaise.

Pesto Mayonnaise

The Tomato Tomato Sandwich starts with a choice of our popular sourdough or multigrain bread, then spread with our Pesto Mayonnaise. Our grilled sandwich specialities also feature a hint or two of the Pesto Mayo.

Simple to make with a commercial pesto as a head start. Peter, the Pesto Man, as we call him, makes ours by combining garlic, fresh basil, and olive oil (no cheese).

1 cup (250 ml) MAYONNAISE

2 to 3 tablespoons (30 to 45 ml) commercial or your own PESTO SAUCE.

Add as much pesto sauce as you wish to give it a good bite of the pesto flavour. Will keep for days refrigerated.

The Classic Pesto Basil Sauce

Makes 2 cups (500 ml).

2 cups (500 ml) fresh BASIL LEAVES

4 large cloves GARLIC, peeled and chopped

¾ cup (180 ml) PINE NUTS

1 cup (250 ml) good quality OLIVE OIL

1 cup (250 ml) freshly grated PARMESAN CHEESE

SALT and PEPPER, to taste

In a food processor, process the basil, garlic, and pine nuts until it makes a paste. With the motor running, add the olive oil in a slow, steady stream. Add the cheese, salt, and pepper, and continue to process until blended. Store in the fridge up to 2 weeks, or freeze.

Roasted Pepper Mayonnaise

One of the other Tomato sandwiches that customers line up for is our classic From the Garden Sandwich (see The Sandwich Board for recipe), which has as its base our Roasted Pepper Mayonnaise. We also use it on our grilled sandwiches. Makes 2 cups (500 ml).

2 cups (500 ml) MAYONNAISE

2 canned sweet red whole PEPPERS, chopped

In a food processor, combine the peppers with the mayo and blend until smooth. Will keep several days refrigerated.

Lemon Dill Mayonnaise

Take a piece of B.C. whisky-smoked salmon, a speciality of Sundance Seafood Company in Vancouver, or substitute your own catch. Provide a slice of baguette to put it on, and top it with Lemon Dill Mayonnaise. It's heaven!

1 cup (250 ml) MAYONNAISE

juice of 1 to 2 LEMONS, depending on size

1 teaspoon (5 ml) plain or grainy DIJON MUSTARD, or to taste

4 tablespoons (60 ml) fresh DILL, chopped, or to taste

PEPPER to taste

Combine all. Will keep several days refrigerated.

Many late nights were spent around the Clement family kitchen table in fierce debate over the name of our restaurant. Some notable discords included The Kryptonite Café, Di's Place, and Jamie's personal favourite, The Holy Palate.

Jean Quinn's Mock Raspberry Jam

Tomatoes to make jam? "They sure do," said Jean Quinn.

Pat Quinn, the president, general manager, and former coach of the Vancouver Canucks and the man who spearheaded his team to the exciting Stanley Cup finals against the New York Rangers in 1994, has a mom who loves to cook. When she told me that you could make jam from green tomatoes, not fried I might add, I just had to try it. Believe it or not, it really works. Here we go:

5 cups (1.25 l) chopped GREEN TOMATOES

3 cups (750 ml) WHITE SUGAR

In a Dutch oven, or heavy stockpot, bring to a boil the tomatoes and white sugar. Simmer, stirring frequently for about 25 minutes. Purée in a food processor until smooth.

Add 1 6-ounce (170-ml) package of RASPBERRY JELLO. Bring to a boil and simmer for about 5 more minutes. Cool, put in sterilized jars, and prepare according to directions.

Note: To make strawberry jam, use strawberry jello.

Sun-dried Tomato Basil Garlic

For a special blue plate pasta, we butter one side of a slice of our sourdough bread, then grill it. Mmmmmmm, so good!

1 pound (500 g) salted BUTTER

8 olive oil soaked sun-dried TOMATOES, chopped

4 tablespoons (60 ml) fresh BASIL, chopped

2 large cloves GARLIC, crushed

Combine all of the ingredients in the food processor until creamy and well blended. Spread about 2 tablespoons (60 ml) on one side of a thick slice of sourdough bread. Grill on both sides until golden. Serve immediately.

Barb's Cranberry Chutney

Barb Watts has been a partner in many cooking classes and seminars over the years and her cranberry sauce has now become famous at the Tomato. Sandwiched between mayonnaise, butter lettuce, and roasted turkey, it makes the number one sandwich bar none. We make tons at the restaurant, this is a cut-down version.

2 cups (500 ml) CRANBERRIES, fresh or frozen

¼ cup (60 ml) RAISINS

½ teaspoon (2.5 ml) CINNAMON

¼ teaspoon (1 ml) each of ground CLOVES, GINGER, NUTMEG

¾ cup (180 ml) WHITE SUGAR

½ cup (125 ml) APPLE JUICE

1 tablespoon (15 ml) fresh LEMON JUICE

Combine cranberries and raisins in a large saucepan along with the sugar, lemon juice, and apple juice. Add the spices and bring the mixture to a boil, then simmer until the sauce is thickened and the fruit tender, about 20 to 30 minutes. Cool. Will keep for a week or so in the fridge, or it freezes well.

With Doug on board as one of the Vancouver Canucks' physicians, I have become a rabid hockey fan. Sitting five rows behind the Canuck bench, we get to see the players' reactions as they come off each shift. It can be pretty dramatic at times. Then, in total contrast, I watch the players outside their dressing room after the game, when they seem calm, smartly dressed, and have the time to sign autographs for young fans. Of course, if they lose a game, the fans usually show respect and forgo autographs. When the players do get time to drop by the Tomato, they go for the power Juice Bar combos or our hearty Vegetarian Chili. At the beginning of the shortened 1994-95 season we had fun hosting a luncheon for the coaches' wives and the wives and girlfriends of the players. Most of the time the Canucks see one another at the arena during practices and games, so the luncheon gave them a

NOTE: You can add 1 cup (250 ml) peeled and chopped ripe pears (optional) before simmering. You can also substitute ¼ cup (60 ml) port for half the apple juice.

Salad *Dressings*

Our California organic greens are enhanced by several of our own creative dressings. From a citrus ginger to a sweet and sour maple balsamic, every taste bud is satisfied.

chance to get away from the roar of the crowd and the grind of hockey drills. The most popular choices at the luncheon were the Sante Fe Corn Pie and the Grilled Open-faced Focaccia sandwich. Fonzie's Brownies topped the dessert requests. We were all so busy chatting about food, the arts, and other things that I don't think the word *hockey* ever came up.

Balsamic Vinaigrette

My all-time favourite, with the unique Italian balsamic vinegar.

1 cup (250 ml) OLIVE OIL, or a blend
of CANOLA and OLIVE OILS

4 to 5 tablespoons (60 to 75 ml) BALSAMIC VINEGAR,
or to taste

1 teaspoon (5 ml) DIJON MUSTARD

PEPPER to taste

Whisk together well. Add more vinegar and mustard if desired.

For variation: Add 3 to 4 tablespoons (45 to 60 ml) chopped green onions or shallots, 3 tablespoons (45 ml) fresh grated Parmesan cheese, and 1 tablespoon (15 ml) fresh herbs, i.e., basil, oregano, dill.

Maple Balsamic Vinaigrette

This dressing tops off the delicious Les Dames Pacific Northwest Salad (see Salad Time for recipe).

5 tablespoons (75 ml) BALSAMIC VINEGAR, or to taste

1 teaspoon (5 ml) DIJON MUSTARD

3 tablespoons (45 ml) pure MAPLE SYRUP

PEPPER to taste

1 cup (250 ml) OLIVE OIL, or a blend
of CANOLA and OLIVE OILS

Up to 1 week ahead, whisk the ingredients together in the order listed, adding oil slowly at the end. Taste to correct the balance of sweet and sour flavours, add more vinegar or maple syrup if needed. Store the vinaigrette in the refrigerator.

Just before serving, heat the vinaigrette in a skillet over low heat, keeping it warm until you assemble the salad.

Note: This dressing is equally tasty served cold over greens.

Our very first Customer of the Month was *MuchWest*'s Terry David Mulligan. Seconds after Jamie hung our brand-new Customer of the Month frame – empty – in walked Terry. As luck would have it, he just happened to have a 5-by-7-inch colour photograph of himself on hand!

Yogurt Dill Dressing

Refreshing, tangy, and low in fat! How can you loose?

1 cup (250 ml) OLIVE OIL

1 ⅓ cup (330 ml) low-fat plain YOGURT

1 ½ tablespoons (22 ml) WHITE WINE VINEGAR

1 ½ tablespoons (22 ml) fresh LEMON JUICE

½ tablespoon (7 ml) WORCESTERSHIRE SAUCE

½ tablespoon (7 ml) DIJON MUSTARD

2 cloves GARLIC, crushed

½ cup (125 ml) fresh DILL, chopped,
or 1 ½ tablespoons (22 ml) dried

Whisk all in a bowl. Will keep for a week in the fridge.

Toppings for the greens (per salad plate):

4 thinly sliced RED ONION RINGS
4 thinly sliced ENGLISH CUCUMBERS
4 thinly sliced RED PEPPER STRIPS

Orange Mustard Ginger Dressing

A taste of the Orient with a hint of ginger, sesame oil, and rice wine vinegar. Very light, very delightful!

Whisk well in a large bowl:

1 ½ cups (375 ml) ORANGE JUICE CONCENTRATE, undiluted
¼ cup (60 ml) RICE VINEGAR
2 tablespoons (60 ml) DIJON MUSTARD
1 cup (250 ml) OLIVE OIL
3 tablespoons (45 ml) fresh peeled GINGER, minced finely
¼ cup (60 ml) pure SESAME OIL
pinch of crushed RED CHILI PEPPER FLAKES
1 tablespoon (15 ml) LEMON JUICE

Refrigerate for about 1 week.

Toppings for the greens (per salad plate):

3 thin ORANGE SLICES
4 thin red ONION RINGS
3 thin RED PEPPER STRIPS
sprinkle toasted SESAME SEEDS

The most common basil used in cooking is sweet basil. It is the variety used in making dried basil. But remember, there is no comparison in flavour to fresh and dried basil. Dried basil takes on a completely different taste. Sweet basil has the charactistic licorice flavour with strong herbal qualities. With the growing popularity of Thai cuisine, Thai or anise basil can now be found more easily in markets. It has purple-tinged leaves compared to the deep green leaves of sweet basil. The flavours of citrus and mint blend well with coconut milk, an ingredient commonly used as a base for Thai dishes. Basil deteriorates very quickly and care must be taken to retain its flavour and colour. Store in a plastic bag in the refrigerator and use within 2 to 3 days. Add chopped basil last to hot dishes or salads.

Basil Vinaigrette

"Where's the pesto?" Our chefs cry out as they run out of Pesto Mayonnaise or Basil Vinaigrette Dressing, or want to prep a new Italian pasta salad. It's one of the basic ingredients at the Tomato.

We use the pesto mainly in our Basil Vinaigrette Dressing for the Tomato Basil Onion Salad (see Salad Time for recipe), and in our Mixed Greens Salad. It's also popular for a blue plate pesto pasta.

The secret to making a good pesto is using the freshest basil available and good quality Parmesan cheese. Take advantage of basil at its peak, in the late spring and summer months, and make your own. Freeze in small containers to have on hand year round.

When you are in a rush, most delis do carry freshly made pesto. However, most bottled varieties don't compare to the fresh.

At the Tomato, our pesto is made without the Parmesan cheese for food allergies or for diets eliminating cheese. You could adjust the olive oil in the pesto recipe to compensate for not adding the cheese. For dishes that require cheese for flavour, add cheese to the pesto before using.

This vinaigrette also tops off our summertime French classic, Salade Niçoise.

1 ½ cups (375 ml) OLIVE OIL
¼ cup (60 ml) PESTO
1 tablespoon (15 ml) DIJON MUSTARD
¼ cup (60 ml) BALSAMIC VINEGAR
PEPPER to taste

Whisk all ingredients well in a bowl. Add more pesto if desired.

Toppings for the greens (per salad plate):

½ TOMATO, sliced and cut in small wedges
4 thinly sliced RED ONION RINGS

Snacks
& Nibbles

Artichoke Frittata *Bites*

These nippy little morsels have been one of my standbys forever for all my entertaining, big or small. Prepare them a day or 2 in advance and just reheat them before serving. The artichoke flavour teases the palate; some think it's seafood. It's fun to keep them guessing.

Makes about 16 pieces, enough for appetizers for 4 people.

3 6 ½-ounce (184-ml) jars MARINADED ARTICHOKES
2 cups (500 ml) old CHEDDAR CHEESE, grated
2 GREEN ONIONS, chopped in small pieces
⅓ cup (75 ml) canned MILD GREEN CHILIES, chopped
4 large EGGS, lightly beaten
6 single SODA CRACKERS, crushed
few dashes of TABASCO or LOUISIANA HOT SAUCE

Drain the artichokes and chop into small pieces. Mix with the rest of the ingredients and pour into a buttered 8- or 9-inch (20- or 22-cm) quiche or pie pan. Bake in a 325° F (160° C) oven for 25 to 30 minutes, or until a knife inserted into the centre comes out clean, and it's golden and firm to the touch. Cut into 1-inch (2.5-cm) squares and serve warm.

To make ahead: Reheat in a 350° F (180° C) for about 10 to 15 minutes or until heated through.

NOTE: For a larger party I usually triple the recipe and use a 15 × 10-inch (38 × 25-cm) lasagna-type dish. Makes about 36 pieces.

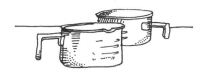

Raincoast's Nachos Southwestern *Style*

Doug and I first sampled a similar dip on our travels to Santa Fe, and I could hardly wait to duplicate it when I got back home to my own kitchen. I used this recipe for my promotions with B.C. Hot House. When I served it at a Raincoast Books bash hosted by Allan and Angie MacDougall, sales representatives from all across Canada devoured it in minutes. They all asked, "It's going to be in the new book, right?" The recipe hadn't been created when we finalized the first draft of the book, but the dynamite Raincoast team were able to squeeze it in, anyway. So for all the sales reps across Canada, this is just for you. Serves at least 24 as an appetizer (cut the recipe in half to serve 10 to 12).

3 tablespoons (45 ml) OLIVE or CANOLA OIL

1 cup (250 ml) RED or YELLOW ONIONS, finely chopped

4 PEPPERS (I use RED, YELLOW, and ORANGE), chopped

6 medium-sized cloves GARLIC, finely chopped

10 small JALAPENO PEPPERS, seeded and finely chopped

½ teaspoon (2.5 ml) crushed dried RED PEPPER FLAKES,
or to taste

2 cups (500 ml) CORN NIBLETS

3 to 4 tablespoons (45 to 60 ml) CHILI POWDER, or to taste

2 to 3 tablespoons (30 to 45 ml) CUMIN, or to taste

PEPPER to taste

juice of 3 large or 6 small LIMES

16 ounces (450 g) solid CREAM CHEESE

2 cups (500 ml) SOUR CREAM

2 cups (500 ml) MONTEREY JACK CHEESE, shredded

2 cups (500 ml) TOMATOES (when in season, use red and
yellow), finely chopped

TORTILLA CHIPS, blue and yellow

In a large sauté pan, heat the oil and sauté the onions, peppers, garlic, jalapeno peppers, and red pepper flakes a few minutes until slightly softened. Add the corn niblets, chili powder, cumin, pepper, and lime juice and sauté a few minutes more to blend the spices well into the mixture.

In a Mixmaster, blend the cream cheese until softened. Add the sour cream just until blended. Fold in the Monterey Jack cheese, then add this cheese mixture to the vegetable mixture, blending well. Put in a shallow casserole dish (I use a 2-inch [5-cm] deep pottery casserole dish that can go from oven to table). Bake at 350° F (180° C) for about 30 minutes, or until heated through. Can be made a day ahead and refrigerated. Take out at least an hour before reheating.

TO SERVE: Sprinkle the chopped tomatoes over the top of the dip. For cilantro fans, drizzle some chopped cilantro over the tomatoes. Provide a big bowl of tortilla chips and let everyone dig in.

Liptauer Cheese

Best described on our Tomato catering menu as "Diane's famous cheese concoction, served with sourdough bread, grapes, and apple. Try it, it's addictive and a party favourite!"

This recipe is for Sinclair and Frederica Philip and their chefs at Sooke Harbour House. Serves about 25.

1 ½ pounds (750 g) firm CREAM CHEESE

1 cup (250 ml) salted BUTTER, softened

1 cup (250 ml) SOUR CREAM

2 cloves GARLIC, crushed

2 tablespoons (30 ml) Hungarian or
Spanish SWEET PAPRIKA

Use only a Mixmaster for whipping the cheese. Do not use a food processor, as it makes the mixture too thin. Mix the cream cheese and butter until just blended. Add the garlic, paprika, and sour cream and mix just until fluffy. Do not overbeat.

Will keep in the fridge for about 4 to 5 days. Can also be frozen. If frozen, thaw and whip slightly before serving.

"Hi, Diane, it's Sinclair Philip calling. Where can I buy the B.C. Liptauer cheese that my chef loved at the Tomato? He's been raving about it ever since he was there." "Actually, Sinclair, you can't buy the cheese. I make it. It's been an old standby recipe of mine for over 30 years." High praise like that from the man who runs Sooke Harbour House with his wife, Frederica, on Vancouver Island would make anyone's day. It's one of the finest inns in the world.

To SERVE: Place the cheese on an attractive dish, arrange with clusters of grapes and slices of apple. Serve with crackers or sourdough baguette bread.

The *Tomato's* Tomato Salsa

Our food processor is constantly on the go making salsa with a good balance of garlic, cilantro, and chilies. It takes minutes to make. Try it, you'll become famous for your very own fresh salsa. Makes about 4 cups (1 *l*) of salsa.

1 medium red or white ONION, minced

1 bunch CILANTRO, trimmed, leaving about 1 inch (2.5 cm) of stem with leaves

3 to 4 JALAPENO or SERRANO CHILIES, seeded

1 28-ounce (795 ml) can Italian PLUM TOMATOES, chopped or crushed

2 cloves GARLIC, crushed

juice of 2 LIMES

½ teaspoon (2.5 ml) SALT

MAKING THE SALSA BY HAND: Mince the onion, cilantro, and chilies. Crush the tomatoes by hand or by using a fork, draining the juice if watery. Crush the garlic with a press and combine with the onions, cilantro, chilies, and tomatoes. Season with the lime juice and salt.

FOOD PROCESSOR METHOD: For the best texture, the ingredients should be processed in 2 batches and combined after. Process the onion and chilies until finely chopped by pulsing the machine. Do not overprocess. Remove from the work bowl and add the cilantro and tomatoes. Pulse to chop the cilantro and tomatoes. Add the crushed garlic, lime juice, and salt. Pulse to blend. Combine the onion and chilies mixture with the tomatoes and adjust the juice and salt. Will keep up to 3 days refrigerated.

At 11:20 a.m. on Thursday, August 22, 1991, I greeted our first customer and sat him in booth 6. This was a surprise to Jennifer and Jamie since they didn't think we were going to open until the next day. "Oh, no," I said, "today's fine!" One hour later we were experiencing our first lunch rush. Ever. The first customer's name was Dane DeViller. He still eats here.

Santa Fe Crusted Prawns *and* Scallops

If you ever get a chance to visit Santa Fe, you won't be disappointed. This historical capital city of New Mexico is noted for its diversity of cultures from its early settlers – namely, the Spanish, Mexican, Pueblo Indian, and the pioneer Anglo-American people. Combine this traditional cooking with the innovative creations from the new breed of talented chefs and you have a gastronomic adventure that will tease your taste buds to no end. Doug and I certainly had our taste buds aroused when we spent a leisurely lunch sampling the chefs' signature dishes at the outstanding Inn of the Anazazi Restaurant in downtown Sante Fe. This prawn and scallop appetizer is an adaptation of the dish their chef created for us.

I once presented this appetizer at our Les Dames d'Escoffier fund-raising cooking class, where it received raves. Our first fund-raiser for scholarships for women seeking education in the food and wine profession was a triumph.

PRAWN AND SCALLOP PREPARATION: As an appetizer, I am allowing 4 prawns plus 4 scallops per person. Because some guests may be allergic to prawns or scallops, I sauté each separately and serve them on separate platters.

32 medium-sized raw PRAWNS, peeled

32 large SCALLOPS

4 tablespoons (60 ml) light OLIVE OIL

SPICE MIX FOR SEAFOOD: This spice mix can be prepared well in advance and keeps indefinitely. Also great on chicken or other seafood for grilling, so make lots.

3 tablespoons (45 ml) CINNAMON

4 tablespoons (60 ml) whole CORIANDER SEEDS, finely crushed

3 tablespoons (45 ml) WHITE SUGAR

1 tablespoon (15 ml) SALT

3 tablespoons (45 ml) Hungarian
or Spanish SWEET PAPRIKA

1 ½ tablespoons (22 ml) CAYENNE PEPPER

In a bowl, combine the spices, sugar, and salt. Put in a container. Just before serving, heat the oil in 2 large fry pans. May need to add more to coat the bottom of each pan. Shake half of the prawns and scallops in 2 separate bowls with enough of the spice mix to lightly coat each piece. Sauté the prawns and scallops for about 6 minutes or so until cooked. Set aside in 2 casseroles in a 350° F (180° C) oven until you complete the last 2 batches.

Proceed to coat the prawns and scallops remaining and sauté until cooked. Add them to the prawns and scallops in the oven. Put them on 2 separate platters. Decorate with wedges of limes, watercress, or cilantro and let your guests dig in.

Serve with the Fire and Ice Fruit Salsa and the Roasted Peppers in Basil Vinaigrette (recipes below). Offer lots of sourdough baguette or country style rustic bread for dipping.

Fire and Ice Fruit Salsa

A great complement to any grilled poultry or seafood dish. Best made a day ahead or early in the morning of serving. Makes about 2 cups (500 ml). In a bowl, combine the following:

1 cup (250 ml) chopped fresh or canned PINEAPPLE

1 cup (250 ml) chopped fresh or canned MANGO

¼ cup (60 ml) finely chopped RED ONIONS

3 JALAPENO PEPPERS, about ⅓ cup (80 ml)
seeded and finely chopped

zest and juice of 2 LIMES

½ cup (125 ml) CILANTRO, chopped

3 tablespoons (45 ml) fresh MINT, chopped

1 RED PEPPER, finely chopped

1 tablespoon (15 ml) HONEY

2 tablespoons (30 ml) RASPBERRY or WHITE WINE VINEGAR

1 tablespoon (15 ml) light OLIVE OIL

PEPPER to taste

Refrigerate covered.

Roasted Peppers in Balsamic Vinaigrette

Edena Sheldon is a treasure. She gave generously of her time and expertise to write the successful cookbook, *Taste of Vancouver: Great Chefs*, to raise funds for the Food Runners' prepared and perishable food recovery program in Vancouver. The Tomato was proud to be part of the campaign, and Edena has this to say about that time: "I'll not soon forget January 5, 1993. While I was sipping a latte in -10° C, my new red wool coat was stolen. I ran around town all day, interviewing my roster of chefs, and freezing! I arrived at the Tomato in the late afternoon, nearly blue. Diane greeted me warmly with a 'Where's your coat?' I told her it had been stolen. A man at the counter was sipping a cup of coffee. He swivelled

The peppers are a perfect balance to the spicy Sante Fe Crusted Prawns and Scallops and the cooling Fire and Ice Fruit Salsa. Makes 8 servings.

BALSAMIC VINAIGRETTE FOR ROASTED PEPPERS: Whisk the following ingredients, place in a covered jar, and refrigerate. Will keep at least 1 week.

1 cup (250 ml) OLIVE OIL

½ cup (125 ml) BALSAMIC VINEGAR

4 tablespoons (60 ml) LEMON JUICE

1 tablespoon (15 ml) DIJON MUSTARD

2 cloves GARLIC, crushed

freshly cracked PEPPER, to taste

3 each RED, YELLOW, and GREEN PEPPERS, rubbed with a little oil

GRILLING PEPPERS (ON THE MORNING OF SERVING): The easiest way to grill the peppers is to line 1 large cookie sheet with tin foil. Set the oven to broil. Place the oiled peppers on the sheet and grill under the broiler, turning frequently until blackened all over. Put in a paper bag and let sit for about 10 minutes. Peel the skin off and remove the seeds.

Cut the peppers into 3-inch (7.5-cm) triangles. Put in a bowl and pour enough of the balsamic vinaigrette over to coat well. Let sit during the day. Drain and arrange on an attractive platter alongside of the seafood and Fire and Ice Fruit Salsa. Save the rest of the balsamic vinaigrette for green salads.

Baked *Brie*
with Sun-dried Tomato Pesto

Sun-dried tomato pesto nestled on top of oozing warm brie just waiting for you to dig into. How much better can it get? I know what you're thinking. Go for it! Serves 10 to 12.

1 7-inch (17.5-cm) round of ripe BRIE or CAMEMBERT cheese, packaged in a box

½ cup (125 ml) fresh BASIL, julienne strips

Carr's Table Water CRACKERS, MELBA TOAST, or thin slices of BAGUETTE BREAD

Sun-dried Tomato Pesto:

Can be made days ahead, store covered in the refrigerator.

¾ cup (180 ml) SUN-DRIED TOMATOES in oil, drained

2 cloves GARLIC, crushed

4 to 5 tablespoons (60 to 75 ml) OIL from the tomatoes

4 tablespoons (60 ml) freshly grated PARMESAN CHEESE

In a food processor: Combine the sun-dried tomatoes, garlic, and cheese. Slowly add the oil until it has a thick-spreading consistency. May need to add more oil if necessary.

Just before serving: Preheat oven to 350° F (180° C). Unwrap the cheese. Place the Brie back in the bottom part of the cheese box. Place the box on a cookie sheet and bake for about 15 minutes, or until the cheese is softened. Remove from the oven, spread the tomato pesto evenly on top and return to the oven for about 5 to 10 minutes, or until pesto is slightly warmed.

Put on a serving dish and sprinkle with the fresh julienne strips of basil. Arrange the cheese on a platter surrounded by the crackers or bread. Provide a spoon for your guests to dig in.

around. Clearly he didn't have a spare coin to his name. But silently he dipped down into the pocket of his well-worn threadbare jacket, fished out a crumpled $10 bill, and carefully, even proudly, flattened it out on the counter. Then he offered it to me, saying, 'Take this. You should have a coat on. You'll catch your death of cold. You can get a coat for $10, you know.' I told him I was okay but thanked him, anyway, tears rolling down my cheeks. Several days later, on my way home, I noticed a church sign at the base of the British Properties. It read: STAY WARM. LET LOVE BURN IN YOUR HEART. That gentleman gave me the best winter coat of all.'"

Southwestern Black Bean & Chèvre Dip

Take an old party standby, update it with a twist of new flavours from our talented Glenys Morgan and the American guru, Martha Stewart, and you have a new hit!

Beans can be prepared a day ahead, reheat to serve. Serves 8 to 10.

1 pound (500 g) BLACK BEANS

2 cloves GARLIC, minced

1 BAY LEAF

SALT and PEPPER

1 canned SMOKED CHIPOTLE, chopped *

1 to 2 tablespoons (15 to 30 ml) ground CUMIN

Mix all in a large saucepan, add enough water to cover about 3 inches (7.5 cm) above the beans. Simmer for about 45 to 50 minutes, or until softened. You may need to add a little more water during the cooking. When soft, drain the beans and keep the liquid.

Mash the beans or pulse in a food processor. Add enough liquid to make a soft texture for dipping. To the beans add:

more CUMIN to taste

1 to 2 cloves GARLIC, minced

½ cup (125 ml) CILANTRO, chopped

½ cup (125 ml) GREEN ONIONS, chopped (optional)

4 JALAPENOS, seeded and chopped

1 canned SMOKED CHIPOTLE, chopped (optional)

SALT and PEPPER to taste

Note: Taste the beans, for a bit of a bite add the chipotle.

Topping:

1 to 1 ½ cups (250 to 375 ml) CHÈVRE

2 each roasted RED and YELLOW PEPPERS,
peeled, seeded, and cut into thin strips **

SALSA (optional)

CORN CHIPS

To serve: Put the beans in a shallow casserole and sprinkle a little salsa on top if desired. Break up the chèvre into small pieces and sprinkle a layer on top of the beans. End with strips of the peppers on top.

Bake in a 350° F (180° C) oven for about 20 minutes, or until heated through. Serve with lots of corn chips for dipping. I usually provide a spoon with the dip for easier digging.

* CHIPOTLE: When the chili jalapeno is dried and smoked it becomes the chili chipotle, dark brown in colour, smoky in flavour, and hot to taste. A little goes a long way. Use sparingly. The canned chipotles are available at most Mexican speciality counters.

** ROASTED PEPPERS: See method under Roasted Peppers in Balsamic Vinaigrette (recipe follows Fire and Ice Fruit Salsa in this section).

Haik's Giant Mexican Quesadillas

For several years I have hosted a party for the visiting guests of the Vancouver International Film Festival. The highlight of the evening's bash is Haik's performance of flipping quesadillas in his colossal cast-iron fry pan. You have to see it to believe it. Haik had it shipped from Germany. It has to be at least 5 feet (1.5 m) wide and 10 inches (25 cm) deep, and it runs on propane. Needless to say, you can do these quesadillas equally as well in a regular fry pan or on the grill. Haik's method: Allow ¾ a quesadilla per person as an appetizer or 2 per person as a main entrée.

Haik Gharibians, the proud owner of the world's biggest frying pan, does not do things on a small scale. When he makes his famous veggie sauce (served on the omelette sandwich at the Tomato), he cooks big-time – 40 balloon eggplants, 40 zucchini, 40 carrots, 6 bunches of celery, 30 green peppers, 15 large cans of tomato sauce, and 6 bunches of garlic. Since Haik already has a day job, he has to do his cooking at night. Usually all night. Late one particular evening, as Haik was loading in his supplies, 2 enthusiastic policemen thought he looked suspicious and worthy of questioning. Haik simply explained himself, then asked the policemen if they'd like to come inside and help chop veggies. They declined.

12 10-inch (25-cm) FLOUR TORTILLAS
3 EGGS, well beaten

FILLING SUGGESTIONS:

Sweet (fun for weekend brunching):

GREEN APPLES, sliced paper thin
CINNAMON
finely chopped PECANS, WALNUTS, etc.
ICING SUGAR
APPLESAUCE

Savoury:

BLACK FOREST HAM (or prosciutto), shaved
cooked CHICKEN BREASTS, thinly sliced
sharp CHEDDAR or MONTEREY JACK cheese, shaved
GREEN ONIONS, finely chopped
canned mild GREEN CHILIES, chopped
SALSA

Use your imagination, starting with a thin layer of 1 or 2 of the cheeses, a layer of meat (optional), a little green onion or canned chilies, and maybe a bit of salsa.

To MAKE THE QUESADILLAS: You will need pieces of wax paper and a heavy stockpot filled with water to use as a weight. Place a sheet of wax paper on the counter and put 1 tortilla on top. Brush with beaten egg and add the desired filling, covering the surface to within 2 inches (5 cm) of the edge. Brush another tortilla with egg and place it over the filling. Cover with wax paper and weigh down with the heavy pot. Make another 5 tortilla sandwiches, weighing each one down when it is finished. Leave completed quesadillas, still weighed down, for about 30 to 60 minutes.

To cook: In a very large, deep Dutch oven or fry pan pour 2 to 3 inches (5 to 7.5 cm) of light salad oil and heat until medium hot. Note: If the oil is too hot the tortillas will brown too fast.

Drop the quesadillas one at a time and fry for about 1 to 2 minutes on each side, using tongs to turn them over. When cooked, pat dry with paper towels, slide onto a heat-proof platter, and keep warm in a 300° F (150° C) oven while you cook the rest. Cut them in 4 wedges, serve with a side of greens, salsa, and Sour Cream Chipotle Sauce. Note: The cooked quesadillas can be reheated under the broiler for a few minutes until crisp.

SOUR CREAM CHIPOTLE SAUCE: To 1 cup (250 ml) of SOUR CREAM add 1 canned SMOKED CHIPOTLE, chopped, and a little of the sauce. Blend in food processor until smooth.

THE TOMATO CAFÉ METHOD: At the Tomato, we omit the egg brushing and weighing down the tortilla sandwiches. We just prep them as an order comes up, making sure not to make them too thick. We grill them on both sides until they are crispy and the cheese has melted.

For the sweet quesadillas, sprinkle with icing sugar and pass the applesauce. For the savoury, heartier fillings, the Avocado Salsa is ideal.

Avocado Salsa

Make at the last minute. A perfect complement to all Mexican food or with traditional corn chips. Makes about 2 cups (500 ml).

2 large ripe AVOCADOS, peeled, seeded, and mashed
1 TOMATO, seeded and finely chopped
4 tablespoons (60 ml) GREEN ONIONS, finely chopped
2 large cloves GARLIC, crushed
PEPPER to taste
½ teaspoon (2.5 ml) CUMIN
pinch of CAYENNE
shot of TABASCO
3 tablespoons (45 ml) CILANTRO, chopped
½ cup (125 ml) SOUR CREAM

Combine everything and blend well. Serve immediately.

Chicken Satay
with Spicy Peanut Sauce

These kebabs are at the top of the list of appetizers on our Tomato-to-Go take-out catering menu. Now, you can make them if you have the time, but we will always be on standby to do them for you. To serve 10 to 12 as an appetizer allow about 1 chicken breast per person.

Chicken kebabs:

10 to 12 raw, skinless and boneless CHICKEN BREASTS
(pork or beef tenderloin can be substituted)
½ cup (125 ml) SAKE
¼ cup (60 ml) pure dark SESAME OIL
¼ cup (60 ml) light SOY SAUCE

Combine the sake, sesame oil, and soy sauce in a large bowl. Add the chicken and marinade for about 2 to 3 hours.

Remove the chicken and set the oven at 350° F (180° C). Place the marinaded chicken breasts into a large or 2 medium-sized roasting pans and bake for about 35 to 40 minutes, or until tender. Cool, then cut into 1-inch (2.5-cm) cubes and refrigerate.

Peanut Satay Sauce

At the Tomato Café we serve this peanut sauce with our Steamed Garden Vegetables and Basmati Rice (see the Tomato Classics for recipe). Makes about 2 cups (500 ml) of sauce. Will keep about a week in the fridge.

1 cup (250 ml) creamy or crunchy PEANUT BUTTER

1 cup (250 ml) canned COCONUT MILK

⅓ cup (80 ml) CHICKEN STOCK

3 tablespoons (45 ml) SOY SAUCE

2 cloves GARLIC, minced

zest and juice of 1 LEMON

3 tablespoons (45 ml) Chinese sweet CHILI SAUCE

1 tablespoon (15 ml) BROWN SUGAR

2 tablespoons (30 ml) pure dark SESAME OIL

SMALL WOODEN SKEWERS

Combine all the ingredients in a food processor, reserving a quarter of the coconut milk and stock. Blend until creamy. If the sauce is too thick, dilute with some of the reserved liquids. It should be medium thick. Serve warm or at room temperature.

If it becomes too thick from the refrigeration, add a little hot water or chicken stock to thin it out.

To SERVE: I allow 1 chicken cube per small skewer, fanning them out on a large platter with the peanut sauce in the centre for dipping. Decorate the platter with an exotic flower.

The first Tomato Christmas party was open to staff and customers alike. The great thing about it was that, almost spontaneously, everybody decided to abandon the incredible smorgasbord and go carolling. We ended up with a medium-size parade of honest-voiced singers carolling their hearts out up and down the neighbourhood streets. And it actually snowed. This became a tradition – the carolling, not the snow!

Mediterranean *Platter*

with Tzatziki and Hummus

This is a mini meal in itself, with Tomato's own tzatziki, hummus with grilled chapatis, and Calamata olives.

Tzatziki:

I like my tzatziki to be chunky and thick. I combine the sour cream with the yogurt, but if you prefer less fat, use all yogurt. We grill our chapatis, but heating them in tinfoil in a 350° F (180° C) oven for about 10 minutes works well. Makes about 3 cups (750 ml).

2 ENGLISH CUCUMBERS with skin, finely chopped
1 ½ cups (375 ml) plain YOGURT
1 cup (250 ml) SOUR CREAM
2 cloves GARLIC, minced
½ cup (125 ml) GREEN ONIONS, chopped
juice of 1 or 2 LEMONS
1 tablespoon (15 ml) WHITE WINE VINEGAR
PEPPER to taste
1 teaspoon (5 ml) DIJON MUSTARD, or to taste
¼ cup (60 ml) fresh DILL, chopped

A day or 2 before serving: Sprinkle the cucumbers with a little salt, place on paper towels, and let stand about 10 minutes. Pat dry. Mix with the rest of the ingredients. Add more lemon juice, Dijon mustard, and fresh dill to taste. I like lots of dill. Refrigerate covered.

Hummus:

I prefer my hummus without oil, so I substitute the juice from the chick peas instead. Makes about 2 ½ cups (625 ml).

1 14-ounce (398-ml) can chick peas (garbanzo beans)
about ¼ cup (60 ml) JUICE from the CHICK PEAS
juice of 2 LEMONS, or more, to taste

½ cup (125 ml) prepared TAHINI (sesame) PASTE

3 cloves GARLIC, minced, or to taste

pinch of SALT

PEPPER to taste

Drain the chick peas, saving ¼ cup (60 ml) of the juice. In a food processor, purée the chick peas, then add half of the ¼ cup (60 ml) of the chick pea liquid and the lemon juice, tahini, garlic, salt, and pepper. Cream well. Add the rest of the chick pea liquid. If the mixture seems dry you can add a little water to make it smooth and creamy for a dip consistency. Will keep for about 4 to 5 days refrigerated.

Vegetarian Sushi
Roll-ups

Chock-full of everything healthy. These roll-ups will make your day. These are the specific ingredients per roll:

1 CHAPATI

2 tablespoons (30 ml) HUMMUS

3 tablespoons (45 ml) grated CARROTS

3 tablespoons (45 ml) TOMATO PEPPER RELISH
(recipe below)

SPROUTS or shredded BUTTER LETTUCE

Tomato Pepper Relish:

TOMATOES, chopped small

red and yellow PEPPERS, finely chopped

fresh DILL

fresh BASIL

PEPPER

Combine all, adding enough fresh dill, basil, and pepper to taste.

While Jennifer and Jamie were renovating the front of the restaurant, I was busy updating my kitchen. Vancouver is packed with restaurant supply stores filled with multitudes of aggressive salespeople, but one such person remains distinct in my memory as unparalleled in boldness and originality. All we wanted was a fridge. First, he gave us several free espressos, then he ceremoniously served us grappa from a scarred bottle, saying it was his own "special private stock." His eyes became misty as he told me his entire life story: two divorces, a new girlfriend, and the hope of one day going back to Italy forever. As he walked us to our car, he took off his shirt and tie to show me his tattoos and scars. We left him shirtless in the parking lot. We did not buy a fridge from this man.

To ASSEMBLE EACH ROLL: Spread enough hummus on the bottom of the chapati to within 1 inch (2.5 cm) from the outside. At one end of the chapati, about 1 inch (2.5 cm) in, spread the carrots, Tomato Pepper Relish, and sprouts or lettuce across the chapati. Roll up tightly, jelly-roll fashion. You can prepare these well ahead of time and refrigerate until you're ready to serve.

To SERVE: Slice each roll on the diagonal into 4 slices. Arrange the slices standing up like sushi. For a large platter I line the bottom with mixed greens and arrange the rolls on top. I allow about 3 per person for a cocktail reception. Try serving tzatziki as a dipping sauce for the rolls. Your guests will love it.

Chapati Roll
with Citrus Chicken and Greens

Another fun roll to do for our Tomato parties. For each roll:

1 CHAPATI

about 1 tablespoon (15 ml) CITRUS MAYONNAISE
(recipe below)

4 to 5 thin strips cooked CHICKEN BREAST

3 thin slices of both RED and YELLOW PEPPERS

about ⅓ cup (80 ml) MIXED GREENS
or BUTTER LETTUCE (in strips)

To ASSEMBLE: Spread enough citrus mayonnaise to within 1 inch (2.5 cm) of the edge of the chapati. At one end of the chapati, about 1 inch (2.5 cm) in, spread a good layer of the greens across the chapati, making sure that some of the greens are sticking out of the ends. Spread a layer of chicken strips and the peppers. Roll up tightly, jelly-roll fashion. Refrigerate until serving time.

To SERVE: Cut each roll on the diagonal to make 4 slices. On the platter, arrange a few mixed greens on the bottom, stand the rolls upright. Decorate with thin strips of the red and yellow peppers.

Serve with a side of Citrus Mayonnaise for dipping if you like.

Citrus Mayonnaise:

For each cup (250 ml) of MAYONNAISE add 2 tablespoons (30 ml) undiluted ORANGE JUICE CONCENTRATE. Keep refrigerated. Will keep a week.

Note: I use either Hellmann's or Kraft's Real mayonnaise whenever I refer to a mayonnaise base.

Italia Kebabs with *Pesto Dip*

Our innovative chef Glenys came up with this combination for our catering parties, colourful and refreshing.

On each small wooden skewer layer:

1 small CHERRY TOMATO, or 1 YELLOW
and 1 red TEARDROP TOMATO
1 thin slice fresh MOZZARELLA or BOCCONCINI
1 sprig fresh BASIL

Arrange on a platter with Pesto Mayonnaise (see Give Me the Works! for recipe) for dipping.

Note: The kebabs are also great with small pieces of sun-dried tomatoes in place of the cherry or teardrop tomatoes.

The Tomato Classics

Tomato's Vegetarian *Chili*

We opened the Tomato with my version of a vegetarian chili and even the most die-hard beef chili fans keep coming back for more.

A meal in itself with its chunky vegetables, packed full of vitamins, kidney beans, and bulgur wheat for your carbohydrates. Our chili has absolutely everything that is good for you.

It was also in popular demand, along with our corn bread, at the Share our Strength Hunger Awareness Week Gala. Share our Strength is a North American organization made up of people in the food- and wine-related industries. Their mandate is to raise funds to support food banks and their related programs. In Vancouver, the Hunger Awareness Week Gala fund-raiser was held at the Hotel Vancouver. Many Vancouver restaurants and their chefs went all out for this worthwhile fund-raiser, presenting their specialities along with the wine merchants' favourites.

All the proceeds went to the Food Runners, Vancouver's prepared and perishable food-recovery program, and international relief agencies. Serves 8.

1 ½ cups (375 ml) dried RED KIDNEY BEANS

4 cups (1 *l*) cold WATER

¾ cup (180 ml) BULGUR WHEAT

1 ½ cups (375 ml) boiling WATER

2 tablespoons (30 ml) VEGETABLE OIL

3 large cloves GARLIC, minced

1 large ONION, chopped

1 cup (250 ml) sliced CELERY, ½ inch (1 cm) thick

1 cup (250 ml) sliced CARROTS, ½ inch (1 cm) thick

1 cup (250 ml) BUTTERNUT SQUASH,
cut into 1 inch (2.5 cm) cubes (optional)

1 cup (250 ml) fresh MUSHROOMS, halved

2 RED and 1 YELLOW PEPPER,
cut into 1 inch (2.5 cm) squares

1 or 2 large green ZUCCHINI, halved lengthwise, cut into ½
inch (1 cm) slices, or use 1 GREEN and 1 YELLOW

½ teaspoon (2.5 ml) TABASCO SAUCE, or to taste

3 tablespoons (45 ml) CHILI POWDER, or to taste

2 tablespoons (30 ml) ground CUMIN

¼ cup (60 ml) each fresh BASIL, DILL, OREGANO, or 1
tablespoon (15 ml) dried

2 fresh JALAPENO CHILIES, finely chopped

¼ teaspoon (1 ml) dried RED PEPPER FLAKES, or to taste

2 28-ounce (795-ml) cans Italian PLUM TOMATOES,
chopped, with juice

3 cups (750 ml) V-8 VEGETABLE JUICE

2 ounces (55 g) TOMATO PASTE

1 cup (250 ml) CORN NIBLETS, fresh or frozen

sharp CHEDDAR and MONTEREY JACK CHEESE, grated

RED ONIONS, sliced or finely chopped

Cover beans with cold water. Bring to boil and simmer 45 to
50 minutes, until tender. Strain and save liquid. Set both
aside. Soak the bulgur in 1 ½ cups (375 ml) boiling water for
about 5 minutes, until the liquid is absorbed. Set aside.

In a large stockpot, heat the oil and sauté the garlic,
onion, celery, carrots, and butternut squash until the vegetables are crisp-tender, about 15 minutes. Add the remaining vegetables, Tabasco, spices, herbs, and flavourings, and
sauté about 5 minutes.

Add the tomatoes with juice, v-8 juice, tomato paste,
beans, and bean liquid, and simmer over medium heat for
about 30 minutes, uncovered, until the vegetables are still
slightly crunchy. Add the soaked bulgur and corn. Check
for seasonings. Cool down and chill overnight until ready to
serve. Make at least 1 day ahead.

To serve: Reheat uncovered until hot. Serve in bowls,
topped with grated cheeses and red onion. This chili also
freezes well.

Seated over in the far corner of
Tomato-to-Go is jazz musician
Barry Merritt, the first customer
of the day. He sits in his
favourite corner spot at the
counter, nibbling on a scone
while sipping a coffee. He seri-
ously scans both of the city's
papers before leaving us with
his usual friendly smile and a
cheerful adieu. His thoughts on
the restaurant: "The Tomato is
definitely not a chain/formula
operation. The personable,
competent, interesting staff
make me feel right at home.
They even open 'earlier' just for
me, so I pitch in and help put
out the chairs at the counter. It's
a unique place."

Santa Fe Corn Pie

A winner from day one at the Tomato, with corn, chilies, and Monterey Jack cheese. Have it Southwestern style with salsa, corn chips, and Tex-Mex bean salad (see John's Tex-Mex Black Bean and Corn Salad in Salad Time section).

Perfect for weekend entertaining at home, on a mountain retreat, or summer boating. Toss a salad while you pop it in the microwave or oven for a quick brunch. Serves 6.

Larry Cordes was the first delivery man to visit the Tomato. He is now one of the Yen Brothers' top salesmen. Always on time, extremely pleasant, and fun to chat with as he munches on a big muffin just out of the oven, Larry is as loyal to us now as he was at the beginning. "Seven in the morning," he says, "is my favourite time at the Tomato. It's when Diane has time to talk to me, either about business or just gossiping about the Canucks. Every time I visit the Tomato is an experience."

3 large EGGS
1 8 ¾-ounce (248-ml) can CREAM-STYLE CORN
1 10-ounce (284-ml) package FROZEN CORN, thawed
¼ cup (60 ml) BUTTER, melted
½ cup (125 ml) YELLOW CORNMEAL
1 cup (250 ml) SOUR CREAM
4 tablespoons (60 ml) MONTEREY JACK CHEESE
1 can mild GREEN CHILIES, chopped
PEPPER to taste
¼ teaspoon (1 ml) WORCESTERSHIRE SAUCE
few shots of TABASCO
3 tablespoons (45 ml) GREEN ONIONS, chopped
1 10-inch (25-cm) PIE or QUICHE PLATE

Butter the pie plate generously. In a large bowl, beat the eggs with a whisk. Add the remaining ingredients and stir until thoroughly mixed. Pour into the pie plate and bake uncovered at 350° F (180° C) for about 45 to 50 minutes, or until golden and firm in the middle. The pie may be baked and refrigerated for up to 3 days.

To reheat: Place in a 350° F (180° C) oven for about 20 to 25 minutes, or until warmed. Place 1 piece in the microwave for about 2 minutes for reheating.

Grilled Chicken *Caesar*

Served atop our famous Tomato Caesar (see Salad Time for recipe). At the Tomato we marinade our boneless chicken breasts for both our grilled chicken sandwiches and our Caesar salads. The infusion of the Dijon mustard and lemon juice with the chicken makes for an interesting tease of flavours. Why did the chicken cross the road? . . . Serves 6.

3 whole CHICKEN BREASTS, boned, skinned, and halved

¼ cup (60 ml) LEMON JUICE

zest of 1 LEMON

1 tablespoon (15 ml) DIJON MUSTARD

2 tablespoons (30 ml) SALAD or OLIVE OIL

Combine marinade ingredients and pour over single layer of chicken breasts in a glass dish. Cover and refrigerate for at least 4 hours, or overnight. Just before serving, grill the breasts for 6 to 8 minutes, or until all the pink is gone. Slice and serve atop a plate of freshly tossed greens with the Caesar dressing, croutons (see Salad Time for recipes), and a sprinkle of freshly grated Parmesan cheese.

David King, well-known Vancouver writer, tells this story: "One drizzly Sunday morning, just after my daughter Hilary was born and my son Jimmy was 3, we walked the stone's-throw distance to our favourite neighbourhood eatery and got there just in time to be the first customers of the day. Upon entering, Jimmy, out of regard for the spotless tile floor, kicked off his shoes and made a dash for the booth nearest to the toy box. The kid was obviously not born in a barn. The Tomato means a lot to me, but one thing comes to mind – the couch around the side where I like to sit with Hilary and share a Popsicle."

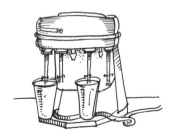

Tomato's Passionate *Tomato Sauce*

This is our basic tomato sauce. We use it as a base for pizza, pasta sauces, etc. It freezes very well. Makes about 6 cups (1.5 *l*).

Did you know that the tomato was first cultivated in Peru, where Spaniards searching for gold came across the "golden apple" instead?

3 tablespoons (45 ml) OLIVE OIL
1 large ONION, chopped
4 to 5 large cloves GARLIC, finely chopped
1 teaspoon (5 ml) dried BASIL
1 tablespoon (15 ml) SUGAR
4 14-ounce (398-ml) cans ITALIAN TOMATOES, chopped, undrained
¼ teaspoon (1 ml) crushed RED CHILI PEPPER FLAKES
PEPPER to taste
¼ cup (60 ml) DRIED BASIL
⅓ cup (80 ml) FRESH BASIL, chopped

Heat the oil in a large skillet. Add the onions, garlic, basil, and sugar. Sauté over low heat until the onions and garlic are softened, about 10 minutes. Add the tomatoes and red pepper flakes and simmer uncovered for about 30 minutes, or until thickened and the flavours have time to peak. Add the fresh basil at the end (I like lots!)

Note: If you have any softened tomatoes you want to use up, just add 4 to 5 coarsely chopped ones to the sauce during the last 10 to 15 minutes of simmering. Adjust seasonings. I don't bother peeling them if I'm squeezed for time.

If you do have time to peel the tomatoes: Slash the bottoms of each tomato with an X and cut out the core. Put the tomatoes into a large bowl or pan and cover with boiling water. Leave for about 30 seconds, or until the skins start to peel away. Drain water and peel off skin. Cut the tomatoes in half horizontally and squeeze out the seeds. Chop coarsely.

Steamed Garden *Vegetables*
and Basmati Rice

When we took over the Tomato Café we inherited a giant wok area with 2 wok pans that would have been a major challenge to remove. Jennifer came up with the bright idea to keep one in use and cover the other one to use as a prep table.

That was the beginning of one of the most popular vegetarian dishes on our menu. We just keep "steaming away." Carrots, red cabbage, snow peas, red and yellow peppers, broccoli, cauliflower, and baby bok choy are the constant vegetables. These are steamed just until *al dente*.

For each serving we put about 2 cups (500 ml) of basmati rice on each plate, arrange the colourful vegetables on top, then sprinkle a little toasted sesame seeds over all. Our customers have the choice of either our Hoisin (garlic, soy, and ginger) or peanut sauce (smooth and nutty), which we serve in a side dish.

Basmati rice:

Basmati rice can be either brown or white, the brown variety being more expensive. It is an aromatic long-grain rice from India and is available at most health food or speciality stores. Rinse thoroughly in a strainer before using. To serve 6:

2 cups (500 ml) white or brown BASMATI RICE

4 cups (1 *l*) WATER

Bring the water to a boil, add the rice, and simmer, covered, for about 25 minutes (until all the liquid has been absorbed). If necessary, the rice can be made the day ahead and reheated in the microwave.

Note: For an interesting twist, use Chinese or lemon-scented tea and, just before serving, add the zest and juice of one lemon and toss.

Cecile Steudel, one of our dearest customers, gave us a tremendous insight into the meaning of strength, belief, and determination that are needed to overcome a major setback in life. Here's how she tells it: "The Tomato carries special significance for me. I was in the ICU with a serious condition. Among the cards was a photo of friends sending good cheer while sitting amid the brightness and good food at the Tomato. Since I'd been a regular at the Tomato, the warmth of that photo was a bit of magic in the confines of the hospital's bleakness and terrible food. It became a goal for me to get well enough to eat once again among my friends. Two months after brain surgery I had the exquisite pleasure of doing just that. Eight more months later I hung my show of paintings on the walls of the Tomato."

Diane's Old-fashioned Meat Loaf

with Garlic Mashed Potatoes

When we first started the Tomato, we hadn't gotten around to hiring a dishwasher yet. During the first lunch rush, though, we realized it would be impossible to operate without one. A confused-looking young man was taking exceptional advantage of our bottomless cup of coffee and quietly vibrating as he scowled his way through a university calendar, trying to figure out his schedule. He drank a lot of coffee. Finally he asked us if we needed any help, and we hired our first Tomato dishwasher. Since then we've had a long and distinguished list of dishwashers, including teachers, stand-up comics, investment bankers, disk jockeys, Olympic athletes, financial analysts, actors, dancers, painters, students,

Whenever we serve my family's recipe for meat loaf the comments are always the same: "This is the best meat loaf, it reminds me of when our mom would make it for us, with lots of mashed potatoes, piquant sauce, and creamed corn." Marc Preston, our day manager, has been our biggest meat loaf fan and is always first in line when we feature it. We actually call it Marc's Meat Loaf Special!

As popular, our Tomato's Meat Loaf Sandwich on hearty sourdough, topped with mayo, lettuce, and tomatoes, is a total comfort food. Makes 2 9 × 5-inch (23 × 13-cm) loafs. Serves 6 to 8 per loaf.

3 pounds (1.5 kg) EXTRA-LEAN GROUND BEEF

1 medium ONION, sautéed in 2 tablespoons
(30 ml) BUTTER until golden

¾ cup (180 ml) CREAM OF TOMATO SOUP, undiluted

¼ cup (60 ml) TOMATO KETCHUP

¼ cup (60 ml) CHILI KETCHUP

2 tablespoons (30 ml) DIJON MUSTARD

PEPPER to taste

2 teaspoons (10 ml) WORCESTERSHIRE SAUCE

2 teaspoons (10 ml) HP SAUCE

few shots of TABASCO

3 EGGS, slightly beaten

½ cup (125 ml) OATMEAL FLAKES, not instant

½ cup (125 ml) MILK

BOWL ONE: Mix the beef, onions, tomato soup, tomato ketchup, chili ketchup, mustard, pepper, Worcestershire, HP sauce, and Tabasco together well.

BOWL TWO: Mix the eggs, oatmeal, and milk together well. Let stand a few minutes and add the beef mixture, blending well by hand until thoroughly mixed.

Divide evenly into 2 well-greased pans. Top each loaf pan with about a ¼ inch (½ cm) of piquant sauce. Bake in a 375° F (190° C) oven for about 1 hour, or until the beef is not pink. Drain off excess juices and serve immediately with the garlic mashed potato, or cool and slice thinly for sandwiches.

Piquant sauce:

Makes about 3 cups (750 ml), enough for topping and to serve on the side.

2 cups (500 ml) TOMATO KETCHUP

½ cup (125 ml) CHILI KETCHUP

generous shots of TABASCO, WORCESTERSHIRE SAUCE, and H.P. SAUCE

3 tablespoons (45 ml) BROWN SUGAR

Mix well. Keeps refrigerated for several days.

Garlic mashed potatoes:

To the absolute classic, add a garlic hit! And to balance the fifties mood, add that old favourite, canned cream corn for gosh sakes! Serves 6 to 8.

8 large POTATOES, peeled and quartered

4 to 5 cloves of GARLIC, peeled

SALT to taste

boiling WATER

2 tablespoons (30 ml) BUTTER (optional)

MILK or CREAMO

PEPPER

Put the potatoes, garlic, and salt into a large pot and cover with boiling water. Simmer until potatoes and garlic are both tender, drain well, and mash. Add butter and milk, and fluff up to the desired consistency. Add pepper to taste.

musicians, and a physiotherapist, but, as I once pointed out, the Tomato is probably the only restaurant to have a recipient of the Order of Canada on its weekend dishwashing roster – my husband, Doug! And one morning, when Haik Gharibians was washing dishes, a customer was overheard saying, "I swear to God that dishwasher looks exactly like my physiotherapist." Marc Preston, now one of our managers, also started at the Tomato washing dishes. He holds the dubious honour of being electrocuted twice in the same day by the dishwashing machine. He did manage to finish his shift and, when asked how he felt, replied, "Oh, ya know, okay. Just a little dozy."

The Tomato *Chefs'* Stellar Blue Plate *Entrées*

O

NE OF THE delights and, I must admit, frustrations at times, has been working with our Tomato chefs creating our blue plates. I compare chefs to the volatile sprinters on our track teams – very passionate, but at the same time, highly sensitive. The two Morgans (not related), Glenys and Allan, have been the gold-medal performers. They were the first to set the trend, with an unbelievable sense of taste, creating soups and blue plates that send your taste buds soaring.

We have been fortunate in attracting many talented, aspiring, and experienced chefs who have shared, and are sharing, their talents in making the Tomato a runaway success. These are a few of their blue plate hits.

Glenys's Green Chicken Stew
with Lemongrass, Jalapenos, and Lime

Glenys is the Queen of the Tomato kitchen. Her flair and fabulous sense of taste shines through in creating many of our most requested blue plates and soups. She's a gem!

This is one of Glenys's Thai dishes that was offered at the Tomato. It drew raves. I'm sure you'll agree.

Marinade:

l teaspoon (5 ml) MINCED GINGER

1 clove of GARLIC, minced

OIL to coat

2 whole CHICKEN BREASTS, boned, skinned, and halved

4 cups (1 *l*) CHICKEN STOCK

2 stalks LEMONGRASS*

4 fresh or dried KAFFIE LIME LEAVES*

1 tablespoon (15 ml) fresh GINGER

2 to 3 cloves of GARLIC, minced

bunch of CILANTRO, roughly chopped (reserve some sprigs for garnish)

2 to 3 JALAPENOS, seeded and chopped

1 tablespoon (15 ml) bottled OYSTER SAUCE

2 teaspoons (10 ml) BROWN SUGAR

1 teaspoon (5 ml) ground FENNEL

1 teaspoon (5 ml) FISH SAUCE

1 RED PEPPER, seeded and julienned

BAMBOO SHOOTS (optional)

Marinade the chicken for 30 minutes or longer. Simmer the chicken stock with the lemongrass and lime leaves for 30 minutes. With 1 cup (250 ml) of the chicken stock, blend the ginger, garlic, cilantro, jalapenos, oyster sauce, brown sugar,

The term *blue plate* originated way back in the days of the early settlers. Travelling across North America in their wagons, the pioneers would establish camp-sites, then get a huge fire going and prepare a hearty soup or stew with whatever they could get their hands on. They would serve it up on blue tin plates or bowls, thus the cook's daily special came to be called the "blue plate." At the Tomato we haven't been able to find a rustic "blue plate," but the food still tastes mighty good on our diner plates.

fish sauce, and fennel in the food processor.

In a pot large enough for the completed soup, sauté the marinaded chicken in oil until browned on both sides. Remove and cut into chunks. Place the chicken and the purée into the pot and add the remaining chicken stock (and more if necessary to cover), simmering 25 minutes. Add the vegetables and adjust the flavours and heat if desired.

In bowls, serve with basmati or Thai rice and fresh lime wedges to squeeze.

* LEMONGRASS and KAFFIE LIME LEAVES can be found in speciality markets or in the Asian areas of your city.

Aaron's Mexican Chilaquiles (Torta)

Aaron Thompson was one of our most innovative chefs. He had a marvellous sense of combining or infusing flavours to come up with unique blue plates that were sheer magic. Once in a while, though, not everyone was up to his adventurous creations. One particular night his blue plate was a wild rice pancake with grilled chicken and a spicy Thai peanut sauce. It was a big hit except with one gentleman who barked at the waiter, "What in heck is this brown thing on my plate?

Aaron Thompson definitely had the flair and mystery in his blue plate creations to entice our patrons to keep wanting more. His chilaquiles – basically a Mexican lasagna layered with all sorts of goodies – are fun to make and fun to eat. Glenys Morgan has now taken over the reins when it comes to creating our unique tortas.

To get a head start in preparing these, go to your favourite Mexican deli or speciality section in your supermarket and pick up most of the key ingredients. This is just a blueprint for you to use your imagination and come up with a torta that will entice. Make sure you press each layer down well. Makes 6 good wedges.

Per torta: Use 6 10-inch (25-cm) whole wheat or flour tortillas.

4 to 6 PEPPERS, a combination of red and yellow, julienned

2 POBLANO CHILIES, or FRESH CHILIES of your choice, julienned

2 small RED ONIONS, julienned

3 cloves GARLIC, minced

bunch of fresh CILANTRO, minced

2 teaspoons (10 ml) ground CUMIN

1 teaspoon (5 ml) CHILI POWDER

juice of 2 to 3 LIMES

OLIVE OIL

¼ to ½ pound (125 to 250 g) CHÈVRE, or a combination
with MONTEREY JACK or SHARP CHEDDAR

1 to 2 BREASTS OF CHICKEN, cooked, shredded,
or slivered (optional)

1 to 2 cups (250 to 500 ml) SALSA or ENCHILADA SAUCE, or
a combination of both

2 cups (500 ml) cooked BLACK or REFRIED BEANS

1 10-inch (25-cm) SPRINGFORM PAN

In a large skillet, add about 2 tablespoons (30 ml) of oil and heat slightly. Add the peppers, chilies, onions, garlic, cumin, chili powder, cilantro, and lime juice. Sauté for a few minutes until tender.

To ASSEMBLE: Use 2 tortillas in the bottom of the pan to form a crust. Begin to layer, starting with beans or some peppers and some cheese. Drizzle over some enchilada sauce or salsa, then place the next tortilla on top and press down. Alternate the layers using your imagination, mixing and matching the peppers, beans, chicken, cheese, enchilada sauce, or salsa.

Top with a border of cheddar, some chèvre in the centre, and a few slivers of peppers. When ready to bake, cover with foil and place in the oven at 375° F (190° C) for 35 to 50 minutes, depending on the number of layers. Let sit about 10 minutes before slicing.

Serve with tomato salsa, guacamole, and Sour Cream Chipotle Sauce (see Give Me the Works! for recipe). At the Tomato, we also serve it with seasonal greens and our Maple Balsamic Vinaigrette (see Give Me the Works! for recipe).

It's not what I thought the blue plate would look like. I don't want it." I came out and said to him, "No problem. You look like a clubhouse man to me. Aaron will get on it right away." After we served him the clubhouse and he had cleaned up his plate, he said, "Now that's more like it!" Then he ordered an extra side of potato salad. The philosophy that everyone who operates a restaurant must remember is: "Our function is not just to feed people, but to make them happy."

Allan's Puttanesca

Allan is known as Big Al at the Tomato. He is tall, elegant, and has a heart of gold. The kitchen comes alive when Allan appears. He is an extremely talented chef and equally talented on stage as one of Vancouver's leading actors. Allan will always be the king of our Tomato kitchen, whenever we can steal him away from the stage!

Puttanesca (pasta of the night) originates from the quaint Italian city of Sienna. This quick dish was popular for the ladies of the night to whip up for speedy energy. Serves 6.

The biggest tomato festival in the world is held every June in Warren, Arkansas. While eager moms enter their daughters in the Little Miss Pink Tomato Pageant, enthusiastic dads munch away at the Tomato Eating Contest at the town's First Methodist church. Meanwhile, at the local park, The Tomato Stomp is a hilarious sight as thousands crush every tomato in sight with their bare feet. Tomato wine anybody? Similarly, Leamington, Ontario, hosts the great Canadian Slice It Right Tomato Festival every year in August. "Slice for slice," it's the best tomato festival around!

⅓ cup (80 ml) OLIVE OIL

5 to 6 cloves GARLIC, finely chopped

1 2-ounce (57-ml) can ANCHOVIES, drained, patted dry, and chopped

1 28-ounce (795-ml) can PLUM TOMATOES, chopped, undrained

6 to 8 fresh TOMATOES, peeled, seeded, and coarsely chopped

¾ cup (180 ml) BLACK OLIVES, halved

1 2 ½-ounce (71-ml) jar CAPERS, drained (optional)

½ teaspoon (2.5 ml) crushed RED CHILI PEPPER FLAKES

1 cup (250 ml) or more fresh BASIL

PEPPER to taste

2 pounds (1000 g) dried SPAGHETTI or FETTUCCINE, or fresh (I usually allow about ½ pound [250 g] uncooked pasta per person)

1 cup (250 ml) or more fresh grated PARMESAN or ASIAGO CHEESE

Heat the oil in a large skillet or saucepan. Add the garlic and anchovies and simmer a few minutes. Add the tomatoes, olives, capers, and red pepper flakes. Simmer uncovered for about 30 minutes, stirring frequently. Add pepper, to taste, and the fresh basil.

Cook the pasta according to directions. Drain and serve immediately with lots of fresh grated Parmesan or Asiago cheese and lots of Italian or sourdough bread to mop up the juices.

Hedge's Mediterranean *Grilled* Sandwich

Heather Vogt's nickname is Hedge (because she loves hedgehogs). Her dedication, positive attitude, and abundant knowledge of and passion for food epitomizes what a superb chef should be. When you find such young talent, coupled with a bubbly and cheerful personality, you have a winner.

With this Italian pepper and onion marmalade topping, you can have a lot of fun creating different grilled sandwiches. Try our Sun-dried Tomato Pesto (see Snacks and Nibbles for recipe) or the Olive Tapenade (see Momma Tomato "On the Run" for recipe) as the base, instead of the Pesto Mayonnaise (see Give Me the Works! for recipe). Serves 4.

8 slices of BREAD, grilled

2 single CHICKEN BREASTS, boned, skinned, and grilled

about 4 tablespoons (60 ml) PESTO MAYONNAISE,
SUN-DRIED TOMATO PESTO, or OLIVE TAPENADE

Pepper and onion marmalade:

1 tablespoon (15 ml) OLIVE OIL

1 tablespoon (15 ml) BUTTER

2 cloves GARLIC, crushed

1 cup (250 ml) RED ONIONS, thinly sliced

1 RED and 1 YELLOW PEPPER, julienne strips

½ cup (125 ml) PIMENTO-STUFFED OLIVES,
or a combination of RIPE GREEN and BLACK OLIVES

¼ teaspoon (1 ml) RED PEPPER FLAKES

½ cup (125 ml) FRESH BASIL, julienne strips

In a large skillet, heat the oil and butter. Add the onions and garlic and sauté until the onions are caramelized and golden. Add the peppers, sauté a few minutes, then add the olives and red pepper flakes. Sauté about 4 to 5 minutes more to soften the peppers slightly. Add the basil. Set aside. Can be made in advance and reheated just before assembling the sandwiches.

To SERVE: Grill the bread. Spread an even layer of Pesto Mayonnaise on one side of each of the 8 pieces of bread. Slice the grilled chicken and arrange evenly on top of the 4 slices. Spread a good layer of the marmalade on top of the chicken. Cover with the other 4 pieces of bread. Cut in half and serve.

We're very liberal at the Tomato, so I wasn't surprised one lunch hour to notice a mother nursing her baby as she nibbled away at the blue plate of the day. Then about 2 hours later, absolutely by coincidence, there was a phone call for me. The woman doctor, whom I recognized as one of the leading authorities on breast feeding in North America, Dr. Verity Livingston, said, "Diane, my clinic is starting a breast feeding newsletter for all my patients, and I was wondering if you could give a gift certificate for a contest we're starting to name

Sue's Mediterranean *Pasta*

A creamy pasta without the calories! Sue and Brooke Godin arrived in Vancouver via Ottawa. Both having extensive restaurant training, they arrived on the Tomato doorstep one day to apply for work, and we hired them immediately.

Sue became part of our grill-and-salad team and Brooke became the master baker. Sue's organizational skills and ability to keep one step ahead of the game made her a key player at the Tomato. She makes a mean soup and her Italian heritage gives her a head start when creating a pasta dish. I always enjoy telling Sue little stories, her laughter is delightful. Sue and Brooke are now the proud parents of a baby girl named Lulu. Serves 4.

2 pounds (1000 g) PASTA, i.e., PENNE or FUSILLI

¼ cup (60 ml) OLIVE OIL

3 tablespoons (45 ml) BALSAMIC VINEGAR

2 large ONIONS, finely sliced

8 cloves GARLIC, finely chopped

1 cup (250 ml) FRESH BASIL, julienne strips

⅓ cup (80 ml) fresh OREGANO, or 1 tablespoon (15 ml) dried

PEPPER to taste

1 tablespoon (15 ml) ground GINGER

1 tablespoon (15 ml) CINNAMON

1 tablespoon (15 ml) ground CORIANDER

4 ROMA TOMATOES, coarsely chopped

1 pound (500 g) SPINACH, chopped

juice of 2 LEMONS

2 cups (500 ml) FETA CHEESE

In a large skillet, heat the oil and vinegar. Add the onions and garlic, simmering until caramelized. Add your basil, oregano, pepper, ginger, cinnamon, and coriander, blending well with the onion and garlic mixture. Add the tomatoes and simmer about 5 minutes more. Add the spinach and lemon juice, simmering until the spinach has shrunk and wilted. Add the feta cheese, crumbling into small pieces. Simmer for about 20 minutes more, until smooth and creamy.

To SERVE: Cook the pasta according to directions and serve in soup bowls, topped with the sauce and a sprig of basil.

the newsletter." I said sure. Then she added, "And we would also like to declare, in the first newsletter, that the Tomato has been named the first 'breast feeding-friendly restaurant in British Columbia.'" So, after taking a deep breath, I thought, Why not? I then recalled when Margaret Trudeau nursed her newborn son in the presence of Fidel Castro in Cuba. The media went wild, and the incident caused a few raised eyebrows. We've come a long way since then, so I was proud that the Tomato could establish a first.

Glenys's Thai Curried *Vegetables*

Another of Glenys's outstanding blue plates with a Thai influence. Best made a day ahead and reheated for the flavours to peak. Chicken can be added. Serve with Thai or basmati rice. Serves 6 to 8.

8 single boneless, skinless CHICKEN BREASTS (optional),
cut into 1-inch (2.5-cm) cubes

3 tablespoons (45 ml) OLIVE or SALAD OIL

1 4-ounce (114-ml) can THAI RED CURRY PASTE*

2 medium ONIONS, chopped

4 cloves GARLIC, finely chopped

6 CARROTS, peeled, sliced a ¼ inch (½ cm)
thick on the diagonal

2 RED and 2 YELLOW PEPPERS, cut into ½-inch (1-cm) cubes

1 cup (250 ml) CAULIFLOWER, cut into flowerets

1 cup (250 ml) BROCCOLI, cut into flowerets

6 to 7 14-ounce (398-ml) cans COCONUT MILK*

1 pound (500 g) FRESH SPINACH

juice of 3 LIMES

½ cup (125 ml) CILANTRO, chopped

⅓ cup (80 ml) PINEAPPLE JUICE

3 tablespoons (45 ml) BROWN SUGAR

In a large Dutch oven, heat the oil and add the onions and garlic. Sauté until the onions sweat and are golden. Add the carrots, peppers, cauliflower, and broccoli. Sauté a few minutes, then add enough coconut milk to cover. Add another can if needed. (You can add the chicken at this point.) Bring to a boil, then lower the heat and simmer about 25 to 30 minutes, or until the vegetables are tender.

Add the spinach, lime juice, cilantro, pineapple juice, and brown sugar. Simmer for about 15 minutes, stirring frequently. Cool and refrigerate overnight, or serve immediately.

* THAI RED CURRY PASTE and COCONUT MILK are available in most Oriental speciality sections of your supermarket.

Thai Rice with Coconut Milk

Usually found in the Oriental sections in supermarkets, Thai rice, or perfumed rice, is slightly sticky when cooked. Canned coconut milk will give it a creamy, subtle flavour.

2 cups (500 ml) RAW THAI RICE

2 cups (500 ml) WATER

2 cups (500 ml) COCONUT MILK

About 30 minutes before serving: In a saucepan, bring the water and coconut milk to a boil. Add the rice and stir. Cover the pot and simmer for about 20 to 25 minutes, or until the liquid has been absorbed. Stir well to blend.

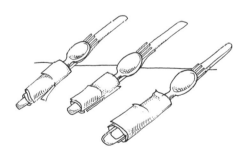

Jared's Samosa Pie

Jared Ferguson has the bluest eyes you have ever seen and the sweetest smile to greet everyone who steps into the kitchen. A talented artist as well as a passionate chef, it was our loss when he left us to open his own café. We are all so proud of him and know he will be successful. A wonderful, caring, gentle young man, and the first of the Tomato team to branch out to open The Hungry Heart in White Rock, B.C. His longtime dream became a reality.

Among many of Jared's fabulous and creative blue plates, he will long be remembered for his outstanding samosa pies. Serves 8.

Crust:

2 ½ cups (625 ml) ALL-PURPOSE FLOUR

1 cup (250 ml) UNSALTED BUTTER, cut into small pieces

½ teaspoon (2.5 ml) SALT

½ cup (125 ml) ICE WATER

1 10-inch (25-cm) SPRINGFORM PAN

EGG WASH: 1 large egg and 1 tablespoon (15 ml) water, whisked together.

In a food processor, process the flour, butter, and salt until it resembles coarse meal. Add the water slowly until the dough forms a soft ball. Wrap in Saran Wrap and refrigerate about 1 to 2 hours. The dough will be moist and softer than most pastry.

TO ASSEMBLE: Leave about ⅓ of the dough for the top crust. Roll out the remaining dough, about ⅛ inch (⅓ cm) thick. Line the springform pan with the dough, letting it hang over the top about a ½ inch (1 cm). Brush with the egg wash. Pour in the filling and press down well. Roll out the remaining crust. Place over the pan, trim the pastry and crimp the edges, sealing well. Brush with the remaining egg wash.

Tomato chef Jared Ferguson has this to say about his experience of the café: "The best thing the Tomato did was to introduce me to so many amazing, eccentric, smart, creative, loving people. As the staff changed, so did the personality of the place. There were smooth times and rough times. Sometimes we got along, sometimes we didn't. But doing the job seemed to weld us together, and I think that in our often turbulent lives the Tomato was a safe harbour filled with caring people. I learned the ropes of my profession there, too. Fresh from cooking school, I was lucky enough to receive so much respect, to see a young café grow, and to learn and work alongside the greatest bunch of chefs and waiters I know. What does the Tomato mean to me? Family, home, Momma Tomato, teamwork, the people, always the people. I miss the staff terribly."

Bake in a preheated 375° F (190° C) oven for about 1 hour, until golden and heated through. Best made a day ahead and reheated at 350° F (180° C) for about 40 to 45 minutes, or until heated through.

Filling:

10 cups (2.5 *l*) ½-inch (1-cm) cubed POTATOES, cooked

4 tablespoons (60 ml) OLIVE or SALAD OIL

2 cups (500 ml) ONIONS, chopped

2 tablespoons (60 ml) fresh peeled GINGER, chopped

4 cloves GARLIC, crushed

1 ½ tablespoons (22 ml) ground CUMIN

1 tablespoon (15 ml) ground CORIANDER

1 ½ tablespoon (22 ml) MADRAS CURRY POWDER

2 teaspoons (10 ml) TURMERIC

PEPPER and SALT, to taste

1 tablespoon (15 ml) crushed RED CHILI PEPPER FLAKES, or SAMBAL OELEK

¼ cup (60 ml) packed fresh CILANTRO, chopped

½ cup (125 ml) FRESH LEMON JUICE

1 cup (250 ml) blanched or frozen PEAS

In a large sauté pan, heat the oil and add the onions, ginger, and garlic. Sauté until the onions are golden, add the potatoes, and sauté for a few minutes more. Add the spices and stir until they are well blended with the potato mixture. Add the cilantro, lemon juice, and peas, stirring well. Proceed to fill the pie as directed above.

Serve with a mango chutney and raita.

Cucumber Raita

A raita is a perfect "cool-down" condiment, popular with curries. This cucumber raita goes beautifully with Jared's Samosa Pie. Can be made ahead and refrigerated. Makes about 3 cups (750 ml).

2 cups (500 ml) LOW-FAT YOGURT
1 ENGLISH CUCUMBER, sliced lengthwise, chopped, and patted dry
2 cloves GARLIC, crushed
¼ cup (60 ml) CILANTRO, chopped
3 tablespoons (45 ml) MINT, chopped
PEPPER to TASTE
juice of 1 LEMON

I won't soon forget one Halloween at the Tomato. There were pumpkins at each table. The staff were in costume: witches, bunnies, cats, hobos, and Jennifer dressed as Jamie. The blue plate special was prepped, the grill was hot, and children were out trick-or-treating on the streets. The tables were full and the orders were in. Suddenly the lights went out, the music switched off, and the Halloween spooks seemed to fill the room. Halloween arrived at that moment. Frantically we scurried around, lighting candles in

Jazzy Gary's Tarragon Chicken Avocado Salad

Gary Thompson, who plays a mean sax, came to us from Toronto after a successful run with his own café. His years of training in restaurant management in England and California, plus his experience as a restaurateur, added a great dimension to our growing Tomato Café. He had a faithful following of fans at the Tomato who adored his scrumptious soups and blue plate surprises.

On Mondays, when the Tomato is closed, Gary put on his favourite jazz then chopped, simmered, roasted, and puréed his way through a day of food sensations, preparing for our busy Tuesday opening. His good-humoured nature, his positive attitude, and his passion for food never went unappreciated and will always be respected. Serves 6.

Salad mixture:

6 boneless, skinless CHICKEN BREASTS, cooked and diced
into ½-inch (1-cm) cubes

3 sticks of CELERY, chopped

6 to 7 GREEN ONIONS, chopped

1 large RED PEPPER, cut into small squares

¾ cup (180 ml) HELLMANN'S or
KRAFT'S REAL MAYONNAISE

1 cup (250 ml) fresh TARRAGON,
or 1 tablespoon (15 ml) dried

SALT and PEPPER to taste

1 head of ROMAINE, shredded

3 AVOCADOS, seeded, peeled, cut in half, and sliced

To PREPARE: Purée the mayonnaise and the 1 cup (250 ml) of tarragon. Combine the chicken, celery, green onions, and red peppers with the mayonnaise. Blend well. Divide the greens among 6 salad plates and top with the blended salad. Garnish with the slices of avocado and serve.

To serve as a sandwich: Choose 12 slices of WHOLE WHEAT or POPPYSEED RYE BREAD. Divide the lettuce between the 6 sandwiches. Top with the chicken mixture and layer the avocado on each sandwich. Can be served with a mixed green side salad and the Tomato's Orange Mustard Ginger Dressing (see Give Me the Works! for recipe).

the kitchen, bathroom, and basement. As soon as we realized we were the victims of a power failure and not some supernatural occurrence, we regained our composure. It was quite the scene: chefs cooking by the glow of the gas stove (thank God for natural gas!), waiters carrying candles in one hand and plates in the other, and customers launching into ghost stories. One particularly imaginative patron thought we had rigged the whole affair to evoke the true spirit of Halloween!

The Tomato-to-Go *Bakery*

OUR SPECIALITY DESSERTS, muffins, scones, and breads are made with the best ingredients and no preservatives. You will not find a "mix" creation at the Tomato. What you will find is baking your mother would create if she had the time. We describe our restaurant as healthful but, I must admit, we do have a few sinful desserts. Once in a while, we all feel like a little splurge of something indulgent, be it an Old-fashioned Chocolate Fudge Cake or a sensuous Peanut Butter Pie.

When we first opened the Tomato we inherited the original 1947 range with a grill, 2 ovens, and 4 burners. Little did we realize that within a few months, we would desperately need more ovens to keep up with our increasing requests for real homestyle baking. As luck would have it, the space next door was being renovated for a future catering business and the owner decided to give up his lease. We grabbed it – gaining another oven, plus a convection oven – just in time to meet our increasing requests for our speciality baking. And so the Tomato-to-Go was created.

Sticking to the tradition of homestyle cooking, our cakes are not fancy European creations, but ones that we all grew up on and still crave.

Mom's Old-fashioned *Chocolate* Fudge Cake

Wendy Robertson, a dear family friend, shared her grand-mother's recipe for chocolate fudge cake for my first book. Whenever we make it at the Tomato everyone exclaims, "This is the best!" Try it for that special birthday or when you crave Grandma's moist, deep chocolate delight!

⅔ cup (160 ml) BUTTER

1 ½ cups (375 ml) WHITE SUGAR

2 large EGGS

½ teaspoon (2.5 ml) VANILLA

pinch of SALT

1 ⅔ cups (410 ml) cold COFFEE

1 ⅔ cups (410 ml) FLOUR

½ cup (125 ml) DUTCH COCOA

1 teaspoon (5 ml) BAKING POWDER

1 teaspoon (5 ml) BAKING SODA

1 8 × 12-inch (20 × 30-cm) GREASED PAN

In a Mixmaster, cream the butter and sugar, then add the eggs one at a time, beating well. Add the vanilla and salt and beat in the cold coffee. Combine the flour, cocoa, baking powder, and soda and beat gradually into the coffee batter.

Pour into the greased cake pan and bake at 400° F (200° C) for about 15 minutes, then reduce heat to 375° F (190° C) for about 15 to 20 minutes more, or until the centre springs back and is firm. Cool, then frost with the icing.

Icing:

2 tablespoons (30 ml) WATER

¼ cup (60 ml) BUTTER

1 cup (250 ml) plus 2 tablespoons
(30 ml) CHOCOLATE CHIPS

1 ½ teaspoon (7.5 ml) VANILLA

approximately 2 cups (500 ml) ICING SUGAR

3 to 4 tablespoons (45 to 60 ml) CREAMO

In a small saucepan, or in a microwave, melt the water, butter, and chocolate, stirring frequently until smooth. Add the vanilla and cool slightly. Put into a Mixmaster, add the icing sugar and beat until creamy. Add enough creamo to make a smooth spreadable icing.

The chocolate and butter will firm up, so make sure the icing is not too firm. Spread over the top of the cake. Add a scoop of vanilla ice cream for the ultimate treat!

Louisiana Apple *Cake*

Pecans add a southern twist to this moist apple-spice cake recipe, sent along to me from the deep South. It's a popular winter dessert at the Tomato. Makes 12 good wedges.

3 large EGGS

1 ½ cups (375 ml) VEGETABLE OIL

2 cups (500 ml) BROWN SUGAR

2 teaspoons (10 ml) VANILLA

3 cups (750 ml) ALL-PURPOSE FLOUR

½ teaspoon (2.5 ml) CINNAMON

¼ teaspoon (1 ml) GINGER

¼ teaspoon (1 ml) NUTMEG

½ teaspoon (2.5 ml) SALT

1 teaspoon (5 ml) BAKING SODA

3 cups (750 ml) APPLES, peeled, cored, and finely chopped

1 ½ cups (375 ml) PECANS, coarsely chopped

1 BUNDT PAN, greased

In a Mixmaster, blend the eggs, oil, sugar, and vanilla until creamy. Meanwhile, mix together the flour, spices, salt, and baking soda. Blend gradually into the egg mixture, then fold in the apples and pecans.

Pour into the Bundt pan and bake at 350° F (180° C) for about 1 hour and 15 to 20 minutes, or until the centre springs back and is firm. Cool.

Turn out on a plate and pour the glaze evenly all over the cake.

Glaze:

1 cup (250 ml) BROWN SUGAR

½ cup (125 ml) WHIPPING CREAM

¼ cup (60 ml) BUTTER

WHIPPED CREAM, flavoured with a little vanilla and sweetened with a little brown sugar

In a small saucepan, combine the brown sugar, cream, and butter. Simmer about 3 minutes, stirring constantly until smooth and creamy. Cool. Pour over the cake to make an even glaze.

To SERVE: Add a dollop of the whipped cream with each wedge. Best made a day ahead. Wrap well.

Grandmother's Gingerbread *Cake*

Maurice Blaise, one of our first really experienced waiters, used to bake his fabulous lemon meringue pies for us. He constructed a special tray that enabled him to carry 4 pies at once. This was a sight: Maurice crossing Cambie Street during rush hour, loaded down with 4 lemon meringue pies, all with his astounding 6-inch meringue. Traffic would stop! Maurice and David Yanchuk, one of our first truly professional managers, established a following of appreciative customers when we started the evening menu at the Tomato. They were a winning team!

Every grandmother has her famous gingerbread cake recipe passed down through the generations. This one is similar to the one in my mom's IODE (Imperial Order of the Daughters of the Empire) cookbook – published in the forties in Nova Scotia. Mom added her own creativity to the original recipe, including applesauce to make it extra moist. She kept it all in the family by using Crosby's molasses from the Maritimes. Interestingly enough, the early gingerbread recipes called for bacon drippings instead of vegetable oil. Makes 12 good wedges.

1 14-ounce (398-ml) can of APPLESAUCE, or your own

1 cup (250 ml) COOKING MOLASSES

2 teaspoons (10 ml) BAKING SODA

3 cups (750 ml) ALL-PURPOSE FLOUR

½ teaspoon (2.5 ml) SALT

2 teaspoons (10 ml) ground GINGER

1 ½ teaspoons (7.5 ml) ground CINNAMON

½ teaspoon (2.5 ml) each of ground CLOVES and NUTMEG

4 large EGGS

1 ⅓ cups (330 ml) WHITE SUGAR

⅔ cup (160 ml) VEGETABLE OIL

APPLESAUCE and WHIPPED CREAM for garnish

1 BUNDT PAN, greased

In a small saucepan, bring the applesauce to a boil. Add the molasses and soda, blending well. Cool. In a large bowl, combine the flour, salt, and spices. In a Mixmaster, beat the eggs until light and creamy. Gradually add the sugar and continue to beat until they are thick and golden, then slowly add the oil.

Fold in the flour mixture alternately with the applesauce mixture. Pour into the Bundt pan and bake at 350° F (180° C) for about 1 hour and 10 minutes, or until the centre springs back and is firm.

Cool the cake in the pan before turning over onto a plate or before wrapping to serve later. Serve with a little applesauce and whipped cream.

NOTE: You can use canned applesauce or your own. If it is canned I like to add a little cinnamon and nutmeg, plus lemon juice to taste. For the whipped cream, add a little cinnamon and brown sugar, or pure maple syrup.

French Chocolate Cake *Soufflé*

This sinful creation is not a cake and it's not a soufflé, it's the perfect marriage of both! One of France's finest chocolate makers inspired this dessert, which is baked until cake-like at the edges but still soft in the middle. When the centre is cut, the soft interior runs out to create a sauce. Choose only the best imported semisweet or bittersweet chocolate for this masterpiece, it deserves it!

You can make the batter ahead of time, divide it among the custard cups, and refrigerate. About 30 minutes before popping them in the oven, remove from the fridge to drop to room temperature. I love this dessert for my dinner parties because it's so easy to assemble and it receives rave reviews.

5 ½ ounces (155 g) imported SEMISWEET CHOCOLATE

½ cup (125 ml) plus 3 tablespoons
(45 ml) UNSALTED BUTTER

3 large EGGS

3 large EGG YOLKS

¼ cup (60 ml) plus 2 tablespoons (30 ml) WHITE SUGAR

5 tablespoons (75 ml) WHITE FLOUR

rich vanilla or coffee ICE CREAM

8 3-ounce (85-ml) CUSTARD CUPS, buttered
and dusted with cocoa

Mix the chocolate and the butter in a metal bowl. Place over a saucepan of simmering water and stir until smooth. Cool slightly. Using an electric mixer, beat the eggs, yolks, and sugar until the mixture is pale yellow and thick, about 10 minutes. Note: This is the most important step. It must be thick and glossy.

Reduce the speed and gradually blend in the flour. Add the chocolate mixture and continue to beat until thick and glossy, about 5 minutes. Divide evenly among the custard cups (filling them right to the top) and bake until the cake is set around the edges but centre moves slightly when the cup is moved, about 10 minutes. Cool slightly and run a knife around the edge. Turn out on an attractive dessert plate and serve with ice cream.

Comfort Desserts

There is something comforting and satisfying about indulging in a dessert that is just hot out of the oven. It's fascinating to observe our customers, snuggled warmly in a booth, as they share a warm fruit crisp or bread pudding. When the rainy season hits, we know it's time to commence our Comfort Desserts. Our Five-Fruit Crisp has become a Tomato classic year-round by popular demand!

Many chefs and hobby cooks are great at creating terrific soups and entrées, but let them attempt a batch of scones or an old-fashioned chocolate cake and look out! Good bakers, like good athletes, come naturally. They can sense exactly when the cookies are just underbaked so that they'll firm up perfectly on the warming tray. Or they know how the chocolate cake should spring back prior to taking it out of the oven to cool. They read their recipes carefully before beginning to mix, thus ensuring they don't miss anything. When reading a recipe, they understand that when it states to "bake for 30 to 35 minutes or till done," you watch it carefully right up to the final minutes, then adjust the time

Five-fruit *Crisp*

You don't have to wait until the colder months to serve this crisp. Use the seasonal fruits whenever they are available, saving the frozen fruits for the winter months. You can make this crisp a day or so ahead and reheat in a 350° F (180° C) oven for about 20 minutes, or reheat in a microwave. Serves 8 to 10.

Fruit layer:

These are the guidelines to the amount of fruit you will need: Use about 4 GRANNY SMITH or NEWTON APPLES, peeled and chopped coarsely; about 2 cups (500 ml) each of frozen (or fresh) STRAWBERRIES or RASPBERRIES, cut in half, BLUEBERRIES, CRANBERRIES, and RHUBARB. There should be enough fruit to fill the glass dish to the top.

Topping:

1 cup (250 ml) BROWN SUGAR

¾ cup (180 ml) ALL-PURPOSE FLOUR

1 ½ cups (375 ml) OATMEAL, not instant

½ tablespoon (7.5 ml) ground CINNAMON

½ teaspoon each (2.5 ml) ground NUTMEG,
CLOVES, and GINGER

¾ to 1 cup (180 to 250 ml) BUTTER, cut into chunks

1 large lasagna-type GLASS DISH, greased

Combine all of the above ingredients in a large bowl. Work in the butter, using enough to bind the dry ingredients together. Sprinkle the crumb mixture evenly over the fruit mixture, punching holes with the tip of a round wooden spoon to release the fruit juices. Bake at 375° F (190° C) for about 1 ½ hours, until the fruit is soft and the topping golden. Be careful not to burn the topping. If it gets too golden, cover the top lightly with tinfoil. Take off the last 15 minutes.

NOTE: Puncture more holes in the topping as it cooks so the juices will thicken.

Apple Bread
Pudding
with Maple Sauce

The ultimate in bread puddings. When we first started to serve this pudding we called it a croissant or brioche apple pudding, and everyone ordered it. When we made it with our sourdough bread and called it a bread pudding, very few ordered it. Now our customers know it is equally as good with either of the breads. I guess the idea of a bread pudding didn't sound tasty. We soon proved it was!

This particular bread pudding is filling, so serve small portions. It can be reheated in the oven or in a microwave. Use day-old French or sourdough bread, croissants, or brioches.

about 6 cups (1.5 *l*) BREAD, crusts removed
and cut into ½-inch (1-cm) cubes

1 tablespoon (15 ml) VANILLA

¼ cup (60 ml) PURE MAPLE SYRUP

2 large GRANNY SMITH or NEWTON APPLES, peeled, cut
into small cubes, and tossed with about 2 tablespoons
(30 ml) SUGAR

according to your intuition. For example, at the Tomato we've had bakers who interpret "50 to 60 minutes" approximately for baking our corn bread to mean exactly 50 minutes, only to cut up the newly baked bread for grilling and discover that it was absolutely raw. Once we hired a plumber-turned-baker who replaced baking soda with cornstarch for our banana bread, put the brownie batter in bread pans, and asked as he put a batch of muffins into the oven, "How do I know when they're done?" I suggested he go back to his former occupation as a plumber. I figured he would be a lot happier.

5 cups (1.25 *l*) MILK

½ cup (125 ml) RAISINS or RASPBERRIES (fresh or frozen)

3 large EGGS

1 cup (250 ml) WHITE SUGAR

½ teaspoon (2.5 ml) fresh grated, or ground, NUTMEG

WHIPPED CREAM

1 shallow 8 × 11-inch (20 × 27-cm) GLASS
LASAGNA-TYPE DISH, greased

A night or several hours ahead: Combine the bread with the vanilla, maple syrup, apples, milk, and raisins until mixed together well. Cover and refrigerate overnight or several hours.

When ready to bake: Preheat the oven to 350° F (180° C). In a bowl, whisk the eggs, sugar, and nutmeg well. Pour over the bread mixture and mix gently. Pour into the greased baking dish. Bake for about 1 hour, or until the dessert has puffed up and is both golden and has a custard-like texture.

Remove from the oven, pour the maple sauce evenly over the top of the dessert. Serve warm topped with whipped cream sweetened with a little maple syrup.

Maple sauce:

1 large EGG

6 tablespoons (90 ml) UNSALTED BUTTER, melted

1 cup (250 ml) ICING SUGAR

1 teaspoon (5 ml) VANILLA

¼ cup (60 ml) pure MAPLE SYRUP or WHITE RUM (optional)

While the pudding is baking: In a small saucepan, whisk the egg and add the melted butter gradually. Add the icing sugar, vanilla, and maple syrup or rum. Simmer on low heat, stirring constantly until the sauce has thickened slightly. Can make the sauce a day ahead if you wish.

Fruit Clafoutis

Whenever we travel to France I order this sensuous custard-like dessert. The classic French clafoutis is made with black cherries and has been often identified as a "sort of fruit flan." It is best made with fresh fruit. I like to combine a mixture of seasonal fruits, or feature 1 fruit. Peaches, pears, plums, or cherries are my favourites.

about 12 cups (3 *l*) FRESH FRUIT, either a combination of peaches, pears, plums, and cherries, or use 1 fruit only

8 large EGGS

1 ½ cups (375 ml) WHITE SUGAR

1 ¼ cups (310 ml) WHITE FLOUR

1 ½ cups (375 ml) WHIPPING CREAM

1 ½ cups (375 ml) CREAMO

1 tablespoon (15 ml) VANILLA

1 large GLASS LASAGNA-TYPE DISH, buttered and sprinkled with white sugar to coat

In a food processor or mixer, blend the eggs, sugar, flour, cream, creamo, and vanilla until smooth. Let it sit for about 15 minutes while you prepare the fruit. For pears and peaches: Peel, core, and cut into thin slices. For plums and cherries: Remove the pit or seed and cut into thin slices.

Spread the fruit, or fruits, in the baking dish. Pour the batter evenly over the fruit, covering all evenly. Bake in a 400° F (200° C) oven for about 35 to 50 minutes, or until the batter puffs up and is golden and a knife inserted in the middle comes out clean. Keep checking from the 35 minute mark on. The timing depends on what type of fruit you are using. It should have a custard-like consistency.

Serve warm, or at room temperature, with whipped cream or crème fraîche.

Crème fraîche:

1 cup (250 ml) WHIPPING CREAM
1 cup (250 ml) SOUR CREAM

Mix until smooth. Cover and leave at room temperature for about 24 hours. Stir the mixture and refrigerate covered. Will keep about 1 week.

Cheesecakes

Everyone loves cheesecake, so I find it hard to believe that there are so many lousy restaurant-made cheesecakes!

When Doug and I were first married, he interned in San Francisco. One of the interns' wives gave me her family's traditional cheesecake recipe. That goes back 37 years, so it must be a pretty mean cheesecake. Our customers think so!

Momma Tomato's Classic *Cheesecake*

Makes 12 large or 16 medium-sized pieces.

Crust:

1 ½ cups (375 ml) finely crushed VANILLA WAFER COOKIES
5 to 6 tablespoons (75 to 90 ml) BUTTER, melted

Crush the vanilla wafer cookies in the food processor. Put into a bowl, add the butter and mix well. Pat into the bottom and up the sides, about 2 inches (5 cm) of the springform pan. Bake at 350° F (180° C) for about 7 to 8 minutes. Cool.

Filling:

24 ounces (680 g) solid CREAM CHEESE

1 cup (250 ml) WHITE SUGAR

4 large EGGS

1 tablespoon (15 ml) VANILLA

1 cup (250 ml) SOUR CREAM

Heat the oven to 350° F (180° C). In a food processor, cream the cheese and gradually beat in the sugar. Add the eggs, vanilla (or other substitutes), and sour cream and blend until smooth. Pour into the crust and bake until set, about 45 to 55 minutes. Do not overcook. The filling should be just firm and the middle not runny. Cool about 10 minutes. Top with the following mixture to make an even layer.

Sour cream topping:

2 cups (500 ml) SOUR CREAM

2 tablespoons (30 ml) WHITE SUGAR

After topping the cake, bake an additional 10 minutes, remove from oven, cool, and refrigerate. Can be made a day or 2 ahead of serving.

CHEESECAKE VARIABLES

Chocolate Espresso Cheesecake

Alter Momma Tomato's Classic Cheesecake recipe as follows:

CRUST: Substitute 1 ½ cups (375 ml) CRUSHED CHOCO-LATE WAFER COOKIES for the vanilla wafer cookies.

FILLING: In the food processor, in addition to the original ingredients, add:

12 ounces (340 g) CHOCOLATE CHIPS, melted

3 tablespoons (45 ml) FLOUR

¼ cup (60 ml) ESPRESSO or EXTRA-STRENGTH COFFEE, or half ESPRESSO and half KAHLÚA or TIA MARIA liqueur

Bake according to directions.

Lemon Cheesecake

Alter Momma Tomato's Classic Cheesecake recipe as follows:

CRUST: Use the original vanilla wafer crust (crushed gingersnaps can also be substituted).

FILLING: Add the juice and zest of 2 LEMONS to the original filling ingredients.

SOUR CREAM TOPPING: Add 1 tablespoon (15 ml) LEMON JUICE to the original topping.

Bake according to directions.

Ginger Cheesecake

Alter Momma Tomato's Classic Cheesecake recipe as follows:

CRUST: Substitute 1 ½ cups (375 ml) finely crushed GINGERSNAPS for the vanilla wafers.

FILLING: Substitute 3 tablespoons (45 ml) finely chopped CANDIED GINGER and the zest and juice of 1 large LEMON for the vanilla in the original recipe.

Bake according to directions.

Banana Cheesecake

Alter Momma Tomato's Classic Cheesecake recipe as follows:

CRUST: You can use either the original vanilla or chocolate wafer crust.

FILLING: Add 1 cup (250 ml) mashed ripe BANANA and cut the sour cream down to a ½ cup (125 ml) in the original recipe. TOPPING: Leave the same amount of sour cream for the topping.

Bake according to directions.

Peanut Butter Chocolate Chip *Oatmeal Cookies*

Our customers of all ages have a frown on their faces when we run out of our speciality cookies. When you just can't make up your mind about which one to choose, our most popular is the Peanut Butter Chocolate Chip Oatmeal Cookie. These are the ultimate chocolate chip cookies. They're everything rolled into one. Lots of peanut butter, chocolate chips, and crunchy oatmeal, with a hint of cinnamon! Need we say more? Makes about 3 ½ dozen cookies

We had a lot of fun hosting the Canadian Athletic Team at the Tomato en route to the 1991 World Championships in Japan. They were a hungry crew who went wild over Fonzie's Brownies. I'm still waiting for a visit from Henry Winkler – maybe one day!

1 cup (250 ml) smooth or crunchy PEANUT BUTTER

¾ cup (180 ml) BUTTER

1 cup (250 ml) BROWN SUGAR

1 cup (250 ml) WHITE SUGAR

2 large EGGS

¼ cup (60 ml) MILK

1 teaspoon (5 ml) VANILLA

2 cups (500 ml) FLOUR

1 teaspoon (5 ml) BAKING SODA

½ teaspoon (2.5 ml) SALT

½ teaspoon (2.5 ml) CINNAMON

2 cups (500 ml) OATMEAL, not instant

2 cups (500 ml) CHOCOLATE CHIPS

Set the oven to 350° F (180° C). In a Mixmaster, cream the peanut butter, butter, and sugars until thick and creamy. Add the eggs and cream well. Then add the milk, vanilla, flour, baking soda, salt, and cinnamon.

Put into a large bowl and fold in the oatmeal and chocolate

chips. The batter will be thick. Refrigerate for about 1 hour for easier handling.

Drop a good tablespoon (15 ml) of the batter onto greased baking sheets and bake at 350° F (180° C) for about 10 to 12 minutes, or until golden. Don't overbake.

Joanne's
Armadillo Bars

Henry Winkler, the Fonz on *Happy Days* to millions, was in Vancouver in the spring of 1993 to direct a film and tasted our brownies at his wrap party. The next day I received a phone call from his wife in Taluka Lake, California, requesting that we Fedex 3 dozen brownies that day to his home to surprise him when he arrived the following day. At first I thought someone was teasing me. But when the woman gave me her Visa number and told me that Henry had phoned her that morning to tell her he had just tasted the best brownies he had ever eaten, I yelled to my staff, "It's for real!" Then the fun began. In a mad rush we whipped them up, packaged them while warm for

Joanne and Jamie Norris are the brother-and-sister team at the Tomato, with Joanne holding the reigns as day manager. She is totally organized, dedicated, and always in a cheerful frame of mind. When it comes to a winning team, she is the captain bar none. Her armadillo bars also deserve a gold medal! Makes 12 large or 16 medium-sized pieces.

10 cups (2.5 l) RICE CRISPIES
½ cup (125 ml) HONEY
½ cup (125 ml) WHITE CORN SYRUP
1 cup (250 ml) smooth PEANUT BUTTER
2 cups (500 ml) SEMISWEET CHIPITS
1 13 × 9-inch (32 × 22-cm) PAN

In a large bowl, mix together the Rice Crispies, honey, corn syrup, and peanut butter. Mix all the ingredients well so that the Rice Crispies are well-coated. Press the mixture down firmly and evenly into the pan. Sprinkle the top evenly with Chipits.

Place in a 350° F (180° C) oven for about 5 to 10 minutes to melt the Chipits. Spread the Chipits evenly with a spatula. Put into the fridge to cool for about 30 minutes to 1 hour. Cut into squares and serve.

Fonzie's Brownies

The secret to these brownies is not to overbeat the batter, treat it gently and it will produce the ultimate brownies! The Fonz would also, I'm sure, enjoy our brownie sundae experience, featuring the ultimate brownie, ice cream, our own chocolate sauce, and topped with whipped cream. *Wild!* Makes 9 good-sized brownies.

8 ounces (227 g) SEMISWEET CHOCOLATE

¼ cup (60 ml) BUTTER

Melt together and set aside to cool. In a medium-sized bowl, whisk together the following (just until blended), don't overbeat:

2 large EGGS

½ cup (125 ml) BROWN SUGAR

¼ cup (60 ml) WHITE SUGAR

2 teaspoons (10 ml) VANILLA

Add the melted butter and chocolate mixture. Blend slightly. Add a ⅓ cup (80 ml) sour cream and blend slightly again. In a small bowl, blend:

¾ cup (180 ml) FLOUR

1 teaspoon (5 ml) BAKING POWDER

Add to the chocolate batter and blend slightly. Fold in another ½ cup (125 ml) of semisweet chocolate chips. Pour into an 8 × 8-inch (20 × 20-cm) greased pan.

Bake in a 350° F (180° C) oven for about 25 to 30 minutes. Don't overbake; they should still be slightly soft in the centre. They will firm up on cooling.

couriering, and then Jamie and I dashed off to the Federal Express office at the airport. They were delivered as promised on time, and since then they've been known as Fonzie's Brownies. But the story doesn't end there. In February 1995 Henry returned to Vancouver to do a new movie, and we got a phone call from California asking us to deliver 12 brownies to Henry Winkler's hotel with the following note attached: "Dearest Henry: Daddy, have a wonderful shoot. We love you. Stacey, Jed, Zoe, and Max." Well, Henry, your Tomato pals love you, too.

The Tomato's Own *Corn* Bread

A hearty corn bread with cornmeal, corn niblets, cheddar, and a hint of green chilies. It's the ideal companion to the Tomato's Vegetarian Chili (see The Tomato Classics for recipe). Also tempting with our gutsy soups! We prefer it grilled, toasted, or warmed in the oven. Don't be surprised by the amount of baking powder. Makes 8 good-sized pieces.

It took a marathon month of testing to come up with the best corn bread for our customers. After 200 pans and 1,600 or more pieces were devoured by our hungry staff and friends, we finally came up with our number one choice. It's a cinch to make: throw everything into a big bowl, watch for bits of eggshell, don't overmix, then slide the result into the oven. In less than an hour you'll be able to dig into a warm, moist, scrumptious wedge of corn bread, Tomato style.

2 ½ cups (625 ml) WHITE FLOUR

1 ½ cups (375 ml) CORNMEAL

3 tablespoons (45 ml) BAKING POWDER

½ teaspoon (2.5 ml) SALT

¼ cup (60 ml) WHITE SUGAR

¼ cup (60 ml) BUTTER, melted

3 extra-large EGGS, slightly beaten

2 cups (500 ml) BUTTERMILK

1 cup (250 ml) CORN NIBLETS (thawed if frozen)

1 cup (250 ml) aged CHEDDAR CHEESE, grated

½ cup (125 ml) canned MILD GREEN CHILIES, chopped

1 9-inch (23-cm) PAN, greased

Preheat the oven to 350° F (180° C). In a large mixing bowl, combine the dry ingredients with a whisk. Add all remaining ingredients and mix until just blended. Don't overbeat. Spoon the thick batter into the pan. Bake for about 40 to 45 minutes, or until a tester comes out clean and the top is golden-brown. Watch the middle, make sure it is cooked. Remove from the oven and cool.

Can be made a day ahead, wrap well and refrigerate. To reheat, place in a 350° F (180° C) oven, wrapped in tinfoil, for about 15 to 20 minutes, or until heated through. Can also be grilled.

Banana *Bread*

We sell tons of banana bread. The recipe originates from a cooking class student of mine, Margaret Rogers. It's so simple to make. It also freezes well, so tuck a few away for that emergency! I never add nuts to this loaf. No one misses them!

½ c. butter

2 large BANANAS, very ripe, almost black

1 teaspoon (5 ml) BAKING SODA

5 tablespoons (75 ml) BUTTERMILK

½ cup (125 ml) BROWN SUGAR

1 EGG

1 teaspoon (5 ml) VANILLA

1 ⅓ cup (330 ml) ALL-PURPOSE FLOUR

1 teaspoon (5 ml) BAKING POWDER

1 8 × 5-inch (20 × 12.5-cm) LOAF PAN, greased

This recipe is made in 4 easy stages. First mash together the bananas, baking soda, and milk and leave to stand. Then blend the butter with the sugar, egg, and vanilla. Sift together the flour and baking powder and, finally, mix everything together, just enough to blend. Don't overmix. Pour the mixture into a greased loaf pan and bake at 350° F (180° C) for 55 to 60 minutes, or until tested with a skewer that comes out clean. Cool and wrap well. Best made a day ahead. Wonderful toasted.

Not only do customers rave about our banana bread but, believe it or not, there is an orange-chinned parakeet named Napoleon who won't eat anything else. Sometime ago one of our customers fed a little banana bread to her bird, and it was "love at first bite." Now, as soon as a fresh batch comes out of the oven, we always make sure we put a loaf aside for both of them.

The Clements'
Lemon Bread

This sweet-and-tart bread emerged throughout North American kitchens in the late sixties when our children, Rand and Jennifer, were tiny tots. They often joined Grampy Bruce for their favourite after-school snack. They loved the tangy lemon-juice-and-sugar topping. At the Tomato, it continues to be one of our most popular breads.

½ cup (125 ml) BUTTER or VEGETABLE SHORTENING

1 cup (250 ml) WHITE SUGAR

2 large EGGS

1 ¼ cup (310 ml) FLOUR

1 teaspoon (5 ml) BAKING POWDER

¼ teaspoon (1 ml) SALT

½ cup (125 ml) MILK

zest of 1 LEMON

¼ cup (60 ml) LEMON JUICE

1 8 × 5-inch (20 × 12.5-cm) LOAF PAN, greased

Topping:

¼ cup (60 ml) WHITE SUGAR

¼ cup (60 ml) LEMON JUICE

In a Mixmaster, cream the butter or shortening with the sugar until light and fluffy. Add the eggs, one at a time, beating until creamy. In a separate bowl, combine the dry ingredients and add to the egg mixture, alternately with the milk, mixing just until blended. Don't overbeat. Fold in the zest of the lemon and the lemon juice.

Pour into the greased loaf pan and bake at 350° F (180° C) for about 1 hour, or until tested with a skewer that comes out clean.

In a small bowl, combine the sugar and lemon juice. Poke tiny holes all over the top of the loaf and pour the lemon juice mixture over. Cool, then wrap well in Saran Wrap.

Whole Wheat
Loaf

This recipe is for all of you who have a fear of making bread that requires yeast. I know the disappointment, waiting hours for the batter to rise only to have a bread that is hard as lead, one that you could bounce off the floor! There's hope for you. This bread never fails and is tasty, hearty, and wholesome. It averages out to a cost of about 30 cents per loaf, which is why many of the struggling college students and athletes bake it by the dozens. It's also known as Irish Soda Bread. You can vary the batter by adding raisins, apricots, sunflower seeds, and a little cinnamon for a delightful fruit bread. Makes 1 loaf, serving 6 to 8.

2 cups (500 ml) WHOLE WHEAT FLOUR

2 cups (500 ml) ALL-PURPOSE WHITE FLOUR

2 teaspoons (10 ml) double-acting BAKING POWDER

1 teaspoon (5 ml) BAKING SODA

1 teaspoon (5 ml) SALT

2 tablespoons (30 ml) BROWN SUGAR

1 large EGG, slightly beaten

2 cups (500 ml) BUTTERMILK

LARGE OATMEAL FLAKES

In a large bowl, combine all the dry ingredients. In a separate bowl, whisk the egg and the buttermilk. Add to the dry ingredients, stirring to form a ball. The dough will be slightly soft. Dust the board generously with the large oatmeal flakes, turn out the dough, and knead about 10 times to cover with the flakes and form a round ball. Cut a cross lightly on top of the loaf and place on a buttered cookie sheet. Bake at 375° F (190° C) for about 45 to 55 minutes, or until it sounds hollow when you tap the bottom of the loaf. Serve warm.

Can be made a day ahead, wrap well in tinfoil. Reheat in a 350° F (180° C) for 15 to 20 minutes, or until warmed.

Here Comes the Muffin Man

Early in the morning we pop the muffin batter into our convection oven, timed to be just warm when our early-morning customers arrive, at 7:30 a.m., at the Tomato-to-Go to start the day with our muffin of the day! I prefer to serve my muffins warm. Never, but never, reheat them in a microwave, it can destroy their texture entirely.

Jen's Power Muffins

The right choice for ultimate performance. These muffins were Jennifer's jump start during her drama school and university days. They are her own creations and are the energy builders for our early-rising Tomato customers and the midday fuel-food for our daytime customers. Makes about 1 ½ dozen large or 2 dozen medium-sized muffins.

In a large bowl, combine the following and blend well:

4 large EGGS, slightly beaten

1 ⅓ cups (330 ml) VEGETABLE OIL

1 cup (250 ml) BUTTERMILK

1 cup (250 ml) WHITE SUGAR

1 cup (250 ml) BROWN SUGAR

4 cups (1 l) mashed ripe BANANAS

1 tablespoon (15 ml) VANILLA

Add:

1 cup (250 ml) each of chopped
DRIED APRICOTS, APPLES, DATES, or PRUNES

1 cup (250 ml) RAISINS

¾ cup (180 ml) SUNFLOWER SEEDS

In a separate large bowl, blend the following:

2 cups (500 ml) white ALL-PURPOSE FLOUR

2 cups (500 ml) WHOLE WHEAT FLOUR

1 tablespoon (15 ml) + 1 teaspoon (5 ml) BAKING POWDER

1 tablespoon (15 ml) + 1 teaspoon (5 ml) BAKING SODA

¾ teaspoon (3 ml) NUTMEG

2 teaspoons (10 ml) CINNAMON

pinch of SALT

¾ cup (180 ml) WHEAT GERM

1 ¼ cup (310 ml) BRAN

Fold ingredients into the first bowl, just to blend, do not overbeat. Fill greased muffin tins to the top and sprinkle with a few sunflower seeds. Bake at 400° F (200° C) for about 25 to 30 minutes, or until a tester comes out clean.

NOTE: The batter will keep in the fridge for 2 to 3 days and the baked muffins will keep moist for the same amount of time.

The Kajaks' Carrot Cheesecake Muffins

Sheila Hutcheon was one of our original Richmond Kajaks' track and field club's middle-distance athletes who achieved national prominence. Her parents, Jean and John, and her brother, Bruce, gave generously of their time to build the Kajaks into the number one athletic club in Canada. Doug and I founded the Kajaks in the early sixties, and it's still one of the top 3 clubs in the nation.

For all of the many thousands of athletes who have been our family all these years, we christen Sheila's muffins in honour of you all. Makes about 1 dozen.

Filling:

½ cup (125 ml) solid CREAM CHEESE, at room temperature

2 tablespoons (30 ml) WHITE SUGAR

1 teaspoon (5 ml) zest of an ORANGE

In a Mixmaster, cream together the cheese, sugar, and orange zest until smooth. Set aside.

Batter:

⅓ cup (80 ml) BUTTER

½ cup (125 ml) BROWN SUGAR

2 large EGGS

2 tablespoons (30 ml) frozen ORANGE JUICE
CONCENTRATE, undiluted

½ cup (125 ml) BUTTERMILK

1 teaspoon (5 ml) zest of an ORANGE

1 ¼ cups (310 ml) grated CARROTS

½ cup (125 ml) RAISINS

1 ¼ cups (310 ml) white ALL-PURPOSE FLOUR

1 teaspoon (5 ml) BAKING POWDER

½ teaspoon (2.5 ml) CINNAMON

1 12-cup MUFFIN TIN, buttered

In a Mixmaster, cream together the butter and brown sugar until light and fluffy. Add the eggs, orange juice concentrate, and buttermilk. Stir in the zest of the orange, carrots, and raisins. Blend well. In a separate large bowl, combine the dry ingredients. Add the carrot batter to the flour mixture. Fold gently until just blended and moistened. Do not over-blend.

Spoon about 2 tablespoons (30 ml) of batter into each greased muffin cup. Spoon about 1 tablespoon (15 ml) of the cream cheese mixture on top. Cover well with the remaining batter divided evenly among the muffin cups. Bake at 375° F (190° C) for about 25 to 30 minutes, or until a tester comes out clean and the tops spring back when touched.

Assorted Goodies

Scones

At the Tomato we have our followers who drop in daily for our English scones, toasted to perfection and served with butter and jam. I prefer Devonshire cream or cream cheese with mine as well. Scones are always best heated, either in the oven or toaster, and never, but never, in the microwave!

I've spent many hours creating what I've enjoyed in England as a truly English scone. By George, I think I've got it! My favourite are apricot. Makes about 10 scones.

2 ½ cups (625 ml) all-purpose WHITE FLOUR

1 tablespoon (15 ml) BAKING POWDER

¼ teaspoon (2.5 ml) BAKING SODA

2 tablespoons (30 ml) WHITE SUGAR

¼ teaspoon (1 ml) SALT

½ cup (125 ml) chilled UNSALTED BUTTER, cut into bits

1 cup (250 ml) RAISINS

1 large EGG

1 cup (250 ml) BUTTERMILK

EGG WASH: 1 egg and 1 tablespoon (15 ml) milk, slightly beaten.

Variations, to replace the raisins:

1 cup (250 ml) dried APRICOTS, or other
dried fruit, chopped

1 cup (250 ml) CURRANTS

1 cup (250 ml) DATES, chopped

1 cup (250 ml) FROZEN FRUITS, such as BLUEBERRIES or
RASPBERRIES

In a bowl, combine the flour, baking powder, baking soda, sugar, and salt. Cut in the butter until well-blended. Add the fruit. In a separate bowl, combine the egg and the buttermilk and beat well. Add all at once to the flour mixture, stirring lightly to form a ball.

Turn the dough out onto a floured surface and knead gently to form a smooth, soft dough. Roll out into a circle about ¾ inch (1.8 cm) thick. Cut into small rounds (about 2 ½ inches [6 cm] in diameter) and place on a cookie sheet. Brush tops with egg wash and bake at 400° F (200° C) for about 12 to 15 minutes, or until baked through and golden.

Marcelle's Low-fat Sugarless Blueberry *Squares*

Marcelle McLean stepped into the Tomato-to-Go when we launched our take-out addition. She came mainly as a friend, but also for the fun of it! Marcelle discovered a few years ago that she is diabetic and has become an expert on changing her old family recipes to accommodate her new dietary requirements. These blueberry squares are fabulous, full of good taste without the sugar and fat.

Marcelle is also famous at the Tomato for her superior wrapping method for all our sandwiches, muffins, cookies, etc. We call it "The McLean Method," and every new employee is taught her style of wrapping.

1 cup (250 ml) WHITE FLOUR

1 ½ teaspoons (7.5 ml) BAKING POWDER

¼ teaspoon (1 ml) SALT

¼ teaspoon (1 ml) FRUIT CONCENTRATE *

⅔ cup (160 ml) MILK

1 teaspoon (5 ml) VANILLA or ALMOND EXTRACT

1 ¼ cups (310 ml) BLUEBERRIES, CRANBERRIES, STRAWBERRIES, or sliced PEACHES, fresh or frozen (fresh are best)

1 9-inch (23-cm) square BAKING PAN

Glaze:

¼ cup (60 ml) sugarless APRICOT JAM

1 tablespoon (15 ml) ORANGE JUICE or WATER

1 teaspoon (5 ml) MARGARINE

Mix the flour, baking powder, and salt. In a separate container, mix the fruit concentrate, milk, and vanilla until blended well. Pour the liquid ingredients into the flour mixture and mix until smooth. Don't overbeat.

Place a 9-inch (23-cm) square baking pan in a preheated 350° F (180° C) oven with the 1 teaspoon (5 ml) of margarine until melted. Swirl the pan until the margarine is evenly distributed. Pour the batter in the pan. Sprinkle evenly with the blueberries. Bake for about 30 to 40 minutes, or until golden brown.

Mix the jam with the water. Heat until melted. Brush the top with glaze when it comes out of the oven. Cut into 9 squares and serve warm.

* FRUIT CONCENTRATE: Available at health food stores or in the health food section of your local supermarket.

Peanut Butter *Pie*
with Chocolate Sauce

Totally, totally rich, decadent, and sensuous! Share it with a loved one. That way you won't feel so guilty. John Ferrie, one of Vancouver's extremely talented artists, exchanged one of our pies for one of his signature fish creations painted on a chef's jacket for me. I love wearing my unusual art piece and he loves eating my peanut butter pie! It can't get much better than that. Makes 16 medium-sized slices.

Crust:

1 ½ cups (375 ml) CHOCOLATE WAFERS

5 to 6 tablespoons (75 to 90 ml) BUTTER, melted

Crush the wafers in a food processor. Combine with the melted butter. Press onto the bottom and up the sides of a 9-inch (23-cm) springform pan. Bake at 350° F (180° C) for about 8 minutes. Cool.

Filling:

12 ounces (340 g) solid CREAM CHEESE

1 ½ cups (375 ml) smooth PEANUT BUTTER

1 cup (250 ml) WHIPPING CREAM, unwhipped

1 ½ cups (375 ml) WHITE SUGAR

Combine all of the above in a food processor, cream until smooth and shiny and the sugar is totally dissolved. Pour into the chocolate pie shell and freeze for about 1 hour. Refrigerate until ready to serve. Cut into very small slivers, as a little goes a long way! Serve with chocolate sauce.

Chocolate sauce:

Once you start making your own, you will never buy another commercial brand. It's so simple to whip up and so luxurious to taste.

2 cups (500 ml) WHIPPING CREAM

½ cup (125 ml) BROWN SUGAR

½ cup (125 ml) WHITE SUGAR

6 ounces (170 g) SEMISWEET CHOCOLATE

½ cup (125 ml) BUTTER, cut into cubes

In a saucepan, blend the cream with the sugars and bring to a boil. Simmer at a low heat for about 5 minutes, stirring constantly. Add the chocolate and butter. Remove from the heat, stirring until melted. Cool. Refrigerate.

Note: This sauce thickens. To serve, melt in the microwave for about 1 minute to thin out.

Momma Tomato "On the Run"

SINCE MY LAST BOOK, *Fresh Chef on the Run*, Doug and I have been fortunate to continue our world adventures – travelling with our athletic teams to numerous competitions, attending sports medicine symposiums, or just wandering on our own to countries and cities we have longed to visit. Taking notes on our favourite dishes and returning home to come up with these recipes has been an adventure on its own. Hope you'll enjoy them as much as our family and friends have at our "tasting affairs."

The Commonwealth Games

One of the highlights of our careers was acting as the honorary mayors of the International Athletes' Village for the 1994 Commonwealth Games. Held in Victoria during August, the Games featured 3,500 athletes and officials from 63 nations, all of whom enjoyed the friendly atmosphere.

As honorary mayors of the athletes' Village, our responsibilities commenced with 63 flag-raising ceremonies to greet the athletes and officials, and hosting royalty, heads of state, and team leaders. For 2 weeks, the University of Victoria became the home away from home for these athletes and officials. We all lived in the beautiful park-like setting of the campus, shared our country's individual ethnic cuisines, and cheered for our country's teams in friendly rivalry.

Producing 10,000 meals a day for 25 days is a formidable task, but add to that the cultural differences of 63 nations and the specific nutritional needs of elite athletes, and it takes on Herculean proportions. The food services at the Village was headed by the Marriott Food Corporation of Canada, with the executive chef, Stephen Simms, coming through with flying colours.

During the 2 weeks of competition at the Commonwealth Games in Victoria in 1994, athletes from 63 of the participating countries devoured 7,587 kilograms of pasta, 600,000 pieces of fruit, and 677,000 slices of bread.

The Commonwealth Games
Banana Chocolate Chip Muffins

Doug and I held many team receptions at the Commonwealth Games, with the graduate student centre serving as city hall. Chef Barb Armstrong and her team did an outstanding job catering our daily receptions. Our busy days started with coffee, juice, and one of Barb's "quick" Banana Chocolate Chip Muffins. I shudder at the thought of ever using a mix, but you would never guess one was used for these muffins. In fact, it wasn't until she sent me the recipe that I realized she had a head start for the busy morning receptions. So for that emergency wake-up call, have a bag of you know what on your shelf, and away we go. Makes 24 small or 12 jumbo muffins.

1 2-pound (1000-g) package BRAN
or OATMEAL MUFFIN MIX
4 mashed ripe BANANAS, approximately 1 ½ cups (375 ml)
½ cup (125 ml) CHOCOLATE CHIPS
1 cup (250 ml) WATER
2 eggs, BEATEN

Combine all of the above ingredients. Scoop into greased muffin tins. Bake at 425° F (220° C) for 18 to 20 minutes for small muffins, about 25 minutes for large muffins. Serve warmed.

The Canadian Club *Coffee*

Our reception hall was known as The Canadian Club, named after one of our generous sponsors for the Games, Corby Distilleries.

Barb Armstrong put together this special coffee for the farewell reception for our protocol and village management team. Needless to say, the dinner was spectacular and the grand-finale coffee, splendid!

To each cup of steaming hot, strong coffee, add:

1 ounce (28 ml) CANADIAN CLUB WHISKY
½ ounce (14 ml) KAHLÚA
½ ounce (14 ml) IRISH CREAM LIQUEUR

Garnish with a dash of whipped cream and top with cinnamon and thin slivers of orange zest. Cheers!

Charmaine Crook's Coconut & Curry *Chicken*

Charmaine and her husband, Anders Thorsen, don't have much time to entertain at home. They both lead busy lives. Charmaine was the silver medallist in the women's 800-metre race at the Commonwealth Games. She has represented Canada at 4 Olympic Games and several Commonwealth Games and is active as a motivational speaker. Charmaine is also co-host of a national CBC television show on cycling.

Hailing originally from Jamaica, she has recipes for many of her mom's traditional dishes. This chicken dish is one of them. For the busy person on-the-go, like Charmaine, it's a whiz to prepare and it's a winner!

In Victoria, the curried dishes were among the most requested from the athletes. I know they all would have loved Charmaine's. Serves 4.

4 boneless, skinless CHICKEN BREASTS,
cut into bite-sized chunks

2 tablespoons (30 ml) OLIVE OIL

1 small ONION, chopped

2 to 3 cloves GARLIC, crushed

1 small RED PEPPER, julienne strips

4 tablespoons (60 ml) MADRAS CURRY POWDER

1 14-ounce (398-ml) can COCONUT MILK

2 medium POTATOES, chopped

1 10-ounce (284-ml) can BAMBOO SHOOTS

SALT and PEPPER

CAYENNE PEPPER

In a large skillet, heat the olive oil. Sauté the chicken until tender and no pink juices are left. Add the onion, garlic, and pepper. Sauté until slightly tender. Sprinkle on the curry powder and gradually stir in the coconut milk. Add the chopped potatoes and simmer until they are tender, about 20 minutes. Add the bamboo shoots and simmer for about 3 to 5 minutes. For extra carbohydrates, add a side of rice.

Chef Rasmussen's Scallops with Corn Salsa

Doug and I were very honoured to host many dignitaries from around the Commonwealth during the Games. We were truly mayors, the official greeters of the athletes at the International Athletes' Village. Among the dignitaries were the Queen, the Duke of Edinburgh, Prince Edward, and the Prince of Brunei, who represented his country as a trap shooter. The security for the heads of state was very tight when they visited the Village. However, the British Royal Family did one of

Athletes from the Pacific Rim rank high in the medal count at the Commonwealth Games. In honour of their teams, talented executive chef, Blair Rasmussen, of the Vancouver Trade and Convention Centre, shares his recipe for his Pacific Rim Scallops with Corn Salsa. He first presented this exotic appetizer at the Winemaker's Chef's Table Luncheon at the Centre. They were a gold-medal winner!

Chef Rasmussen made the following comments about this delicious appetizer: "I like this dish because of its West Coast theme and Pacific flavour. I discovered the connection between shellfish and corn when I was in Japan, where I had snow crab cooked in corn broth – delicious! The sake is a little tip of the hat to that experience. I feel that the combination with the walnut oil cries out for a fine oak-aged Chardonnay. The buttery, nutty taste of that style of wine is excellent with this shellfish. So to all the athletes of our Pacific Rim and Down Under, enjoy!"

2.2 pounds (1 kg) fresh SCALLOPS in the shell

½ cup (125 ml) SAKE

1 green ONION or SCALLION, chopped

1 SHALLOT, peeled and cut into thin strips

¼ clove of GARLIC, minced extra fine

1 ear of fresh CORN ON THE COB

2 ROMA TOMATOES

1 teaspoon (5 ml) fresh LIME JUICE

1 tablespoon (15 ml) CILANTRO, coarsely chopped

pinch of SALT and PEPPER

1 tablespoon (15 ml) WALNUT OIL

The salsa:

Peel the tomatoes, remove the seeds, and chop coarsely. Remove the corn niblets from the cob and boil in a small amount of water until cooked. Add the corn, shallots, garlic, lime juice, and cilantro to the tomatoes. Taste a little to see how much salt and fresh-cracked pepper is needed to season. Fold in the walnut oil last.

NOTE: A little of the cool poaching liquor (see below) can be added to the salsa to increase moisture.

The scallops:

Wash and scrub the scallops in fresh water and drain. Place the scallion and sake in a large sauté pan, large enough to hold the scallops. (Don't forget they need room to open up.) Bring to a boil. Add the scallops and cover the pan. The scallops will take about 2 minutes to cook. Remove them from the pan when the shells have opened and the meat has loosened from the shells. Pour the poaching liquor over them and allow them to cool. When they are cool enough to touch, snap the shells in half at the hinge and arrange each scallop on a half-shell and place on a platter in rows. Cover with plastic wrap.

When ready to serve: Unwrap the scallops and spoon a little of the salsa on each. Sprinkle with a little more cilantro and allow to sit for about 30 minutes before serving.

NOTE: Use only closed scallops of impeccable freshness.

their walkabouts with us as the athletes lined up throughout the Village to chat with them. That was certainly one of my highlights during the whole affair! Another great moment was having former world champion milers Sir Roger Bannister and John Landy, the first men to break the 4-minute mile barrier, and the great Kenyan runner Kip Keno join us at our Village receptions and at the athletic stadium to cheer on our respective teams.

The *Romance* of France: Olive *Tapenade*

One of our more relaxed holidays was our visit to southern France, in the area of Provence. Eileen Dwillies, food consultant and TV host, and her husband Paul have restored a *petite maison* there. Doug, my brother David, and his wife Dianne spent a fabulous week at their home. It is surrounded by vineyards, olive groves, and lavender fields. Eileen conducts week-long cooking classes there, using the plentiful foods of the region. Meanwhile, Paul drives the participants to tiny hillside villages, wine caves, and outdoor markets, travelling through the poppy-strewn, lavender-scented fields. Their house is also a peaceful bed-and-breakfast haven for travellers from Canada and the United States.

Olives are abundant in their region, and Eileen shares her recipe for tapenade, the popular appetizer spread. Tapenade is a highly-flavoured purée from Provence consisting of olives, garlic, and olive oil. Some cooks like to add anchovies and/or capers. Feel free to add or subtract according to your taste.

Served as a spread for crisp crackers or over baked white fish, as a topping for hard-boiled eggs, or stirred into hot pasta, the use of this delicious accompaniment is endless. Because we cannot easily get the French olives here in Canada, use any good pitted black olive. Makes 1 cup (250 ml).

1 cup (250 ml) pitted BLACK OLIVES

5 cloves GARLIC, peeled

4 ANCHOVY FILLETS (optional)

2 tablespoons (30 ml) drained CAPERS (optional)

½ cup (125 ml) OLIVE OIL

PEPPER to taste

Put the olives, garlic, anchovies, and capers in a food processor. Pulse to mix. With the machine running, slowly add the olive oil until the mixture forms a medium to fine purée. Season with pepper. Tapenade can be stored, covered, in the refrigerator for up to 5 days.

Basil Roast
Chicken
with Garlic Sauce

When *B.C. Home* magazine asked me to do their first food feature with the emphasis on healthier eating, the challenge was to take classic French dishes laden with cream, butter, and cheese and create low-fat alternatives. But they had to have intense flavour and taste. Basil Roast Chicken with Garlic Sauce is what I came up with.

Yes, there are 40 cloves of garlic in this recipe. Garlic sweetens as it roasts and when puréed becomes a perfect creamy base for the sauce. Even the non-garlic fans admitted they were actually pleasantly surprised by how mellow and tasty it was.

Serve with our Vegetable Gratin (the following recipe) and a rustic country bread. Serves 6 to 8.

2 3 ½-pound (1 ¾-kg) CHICKENS (preferably free-range),
cleaned (run finger under skin to loosen)

3 tablespoons (45 ml) dried BASIL

SALT and PEPPER to taste

1 cup (250 ml) fresh BASIL

½ cup (125 ml) dry WHITE WINE

40 large cloves GARLIC, peeled

1 cup (250 ml) CHICKEN STOCK

1 cup (250 ml) fresh BASIL, julienned

Put half of the dried basil under the skin of each chicken. Rub the remaining basil over top. Season with salt and pepper. Place breast side-up in a roasting pan. Roast 15 minutes at 400° F (200° C), then reduce heat to 350° F (180° C). Add the garlic and baste both the garlic and chicken with the pan juices.

Roast for 15 minutes more, pour over the wine, and roast another 60 to 70 minutes, or until tender and there are no pink juices. Remove the chickens and pour the pan juices and garlic into a food processor. Add 1 cup (250 ml) chicken stock, purée, and strain, pressing the garlic with the back of a spoon into a saucepan. Simmer about 10 minutes to thicken slightly. Add the fresh basil and more pepper to taste. You may want to add more chicken stock and a little wine to give you more sauce.

To serve: Cut the chicken into serving pieces, pour over the sauce, and decorate with fresh basil leaves.

Vegetable *Gratin*

Low in fat, high in taste and colour. The joy of this dish is that you won't have a stove full of pots and pans cooking vegetables. Make this ahead, layer it all in an attractive pottery casserole, and pop it in the oven! Great with grilled salmon or chicken. Serves 6.

8 small red or white POTATOES, thinly sliced

2 small ZUCCHINI, thinly sliced

7 ROMA TOMATOES, thinly sliced

6 tablespoons (90 ml) freshly grated PARMESAN CHEESE

dried OREGANO and BASIL, to taste

⅓ cup (80 ml) fresh BASIL, chopped

⅓ cup (80 ml) CHICKEN STOCK

OLIVE OIL

Line a large, oiled, shallow casserole dish with alternate slices of potato, zucchini, and tomato slices. Sprinkle with cheese and herbs. Drizzle over a little oil. Repeat one more layer, ending with cheese and herbs, and drizzle the chicken stock over the top. Bake at 400° F (200° C) for about 40 to 45 minutes, or until the potatoes are tender. Serve immediately, or refrigerate and reheat at 350° F (180° C) for about 30 minutes, or until warm. Cover with a sheet of tinfoil if it becomes too brown.

We had the privilege of attending the private Royal dinner hosted by Prime Minister Jean Chrétien and Premier Mike Harcourt at Government House in Victoria during the Commonwealth Games. The menu was truly "fit for a queen": mesclun salad with avocados, sea asparagus, and West Coast shrimp teriyaki and ginger dressing; roast Saltspring Island lamb with baby vegetables; polenta with blue cheese; ice-cream bombe Victoria; and Summerhill Pinot Noir 1993.

Santa Fe Chicken *Salad*

One of the most interesting places we have visited, Santa Fe, New Mexico, is a city of mixed cultures – the Pueblo Indian, Spanish, Mexican, and the pioneer Anglo-American people all call it their home. The city's cultural diversity is also reflected in its cuisine. It's a city steeped in American history and a haven for world-renowned chefs whose restaurants are among the most celebrated in North America.

Santa Fe Chicken Salad reflects the personality of Southwestern cuisine. It's popular at the Tomato during our summer season, when you feel like a salad that is full of texture with a little bite to it. We call it our "teaser salad." Perfect for patio parties. Serves 6 to 8.

4 cups (1 *l*) cooked CHICKEN, cubed or shredded

1 red ONION, thinly sliced

2 cups (500 ml) MONTEREY JACK CHEESE, shredded

1 4-ounce (114-ml) can GREEN CHILIES, chopped

1 bunch CILANTRO, stems removed and chopped

¾ to 1 cup (180 to 250 ml) BLACK OLIVES, e.g., Calamata

1 RED and 1 YELLOW PEPPER, thin julienne strips

1 to 2 heads ROMAINE LETTUCE
or MIXED GREENS, shredded

6 ROMA TOMATOES, cut into quarters

TORTILLA CHIPS for garnish

Jalapeno cream dressing:

2 cups (500 ml) SOUR CREAM

1 cup (250 ml) MAYONNAISE

3 tablespoons (45 ml) CUMIN POWDER, or to taste

juice of 2 to 3 large LIMES

2 to 3 JALAPENOS, seeded and finely chopped

Combine the dressing ingredients and chill.

To SERVE: Toss all of the salad ingredients with the dressing, leaving out the lettuce, tomatoes, and tortillas. Line a platter with the lettuce and top with the chicken mixture. Garnish with the tomato wedges and tortilla chips around the edge.

Piñon *(Pine Nut)* Caramel *Ice Cream*

This is an unusual ice cream with toasted pine nuts, caramel sauce, and a hint of cinnamon. This is a shortened, fast adaptation of the one we had in Santa Fe. Serves 6.

6 cups (1½ *l*) VANILLA ICE CREAM
1 cup (250 ml) CARAMEL SAUCE (Mexican variety is best) *
1 tablespoon (15 ml) CINNAMON
1 cup (250 ml) PINE NUTS, toasted
additional CARAMEL SAUCE and PINE NUTS for garnish

A day or 2 ahead, soften the ice cream slightly in a bowl. Fold in the caramel sauce, cinnamon, and pine nuts. Pour into an ice cream tray or container and freeze until ready to serve.

Toast the pine nuts on a baking sheet at 350° F (180° C) for about 6 to 8 minutes, or until golden. Don't over-brown or they will become bitter!

To SERVE: Place in ice cream dishes, top with a little more caramel sauce and sprinkle with a few pine nuts.

* Can be found in Mexican speciality stores.

Christmas in November at Chateau Whistler

No matter how much Doug and I travel throughout the world, whenever our plane descends over the mountains of British Columbia, then over Stanley Park and on to a safe landing, we both feel that warm, home-again feeling. Vancouver is truly one of the most beautiful cities in the world. Travelling is adventurous, but we really just have to hop in our cars to enjoy a 2½-hour scenic drive to Whistler, one of the most popular ski resorts in the world.

So when Laurie Cooper, the energetic public relations coordinator at the romantic and fabulous Chateau Whistler Resort, invited Doug and I to be part of a worthwhile fund-raiser, we didn't hesitate to accept. It was a combined effort with the Chateau, the *Vancouver Sun*, and UTV to raise funds to support the Kid Safe Program throughout British Columbia.

When we arrived we were greeted with a fresh snowfall to set the mood of Christmas in November. With an outstanding weekend-holiday menu – presented by one of North America's top chefs, Bernard Casavant, the warm, elegant ambiance of the Chateau, and the superb hotel service, we were truly pampered in style.

Our contribution to the event was for me to do a fun cooking class featuring Christmas goodies and for Doug to lead a power-walk in the early morning to start the guests off with a bang. Did it ever! As they trekked around Whistler knee-deep in snow, the guests enjoyed making snow angels and breathing in the fresh, mountain air.

While we were at Chateau Whistler, chef Casavant revealed his secrets to the best turkey stuffing I've ever tasted. Here's the recipe!

The Tomato has begun its quest for world domination. People have been spotted wearing Tomato T-shirts in Mexico, and there have been reports of them being sighted in such exotic locations as Thailand, Guatemala, and Japan.

Turkey Stuffing "Château Style"

According to chef Casavant, "The difference between stuffing and dressing is very much like the age-old adage, which came first, the chicken or the egg? Today the terms are often used interchangeably, although many people insist there is a difference. That's fine – beauty is in the eye of the beholder!" Makes 14 servings (about 18 cups).

14 ounces (398 g) BROWN BREAD,
cut into ¾-inch (2-cm) cubes

1 pound (500 g) ITALIAN SAUSAGE, casing removed

½ pound (250 g) BACON, sliced into ½-inch (1-cm) pieces

¼ cup (60 ml) BUTTER

about 3 large LEEKS (white and light-green
parts only), sliced (about 6 cups)

1 large ONION, peeled and diced into ½-inch (1-cm) pieces

2 CARROTS, peeled and diced into ½-inch (1-cm) pieces

2 cups (500 ml) CELERY, diced into ½-inch (1-cm) pieces,
including leaves

2 cups (500 ml) DRIED PRUNES, roughly chopped

1 cup (250 ml) DRIED APRICOTS, roughly chopped

6 tablespoons (90 ml) fresh THYME,
or 2 tablespoons (30 ml) dry

1 ⅓ (330 ml) CHICKEN STOCK

½ cup (125 ml) PECANS (optional)

½ cup (125 ml) PINE NUTS (optional)

SALT and PEPPER, to taste

3 EGGS, beaten

Place the bread cubes on 2 baking sheets and bake for 15 minutes, then cool separately. In a large sauté pan, cook the bacon and sausage until slightly golden, about 10 minutes, stirring frequently. With a slotted spoon, remove and keep warm. Drain the remaining fat and melt the butter in the same pan. Add in the leeks, onion, carrots, and celery and sauté until the leeks are soft, about 8 minutes. Mix in the fresh herbs, dried fruit, and nuts. Add this mixture to the bread, then mix thoroughly, but carefully. This can be done a day ahead, allow to cool, cover, and refrigerate.

To finish, add in the eggs and season with salt and pepper, to taste. Add in the chicken stock until moistened to your liking. Finish as per your favourite method. If baking in a terrine or loaf pan, bake in a preheated, 350° F (180° C) oven for 45 minutes, covered, and then remove tinfoil and brown for another 15 minutes.

A Weekend Getaway at Hastings House

Just a ferry trip away lies the world-renowned Relais and Chateaux Hastings House, on Saltspring Island, where you can experience a bit of heaven on earth. Doug and I had a thoroughly relaxing weekend in the tranquil farm setting of this gracious country inn and with the total pampering of the innovative and talented managing chef, Ian Cowley. It's no wonder they have won international awards for personal service and for their attention to detail. Excellence is personified at Hastings House.

Chef Ian Cowley and his creative team spoiled us entirely the whole weekend with such specialities as the famous Saltspring Lamb, Cured Gulf Island Salmon, Grilled Pacific Bass, Sweet Pepper Coulis, Peppered B.C. Venison Loin, deliciously prepared asparagus, island chanterelles, and spiced cranberries, and, finally, an out-of-this-world Candied Lemon Soufflé as the grand finale. Ian shares his recipe for this memorable soufflé with us.

Chef Cowley's Candied Lemon *Soufflé*

A soufflé is really simple to make and it creates a dramatic scene to top off an evening of exquisite dining. Serves 4.

Pastry cream:

¾ cup (180 ml) MILK
1 teaspoon (5 ml) VANILLA EXTRACT
2 tablespoons (30 ml) SUGAR
4 EGG YOLKS
1 ½ tablespoons (22 ml) CORNSTARCH

Beat the egg yolks and combine with the milk, sugar, and

vanilla extract. Place the mixture in a saucepan and warm to a simmer, but *do not boil*. In a separate bowl, add a little of this mixture to the cornstarch and stir to a paste. Add this paste to the warm milk and whisk in. Continue to stir over medium heat until the mixture thickens. Cool and refrigerate.

Soufflé:

6 EGG YOLKS

8 EGG WHITES

2 ounces (58 g) PASTRY CREAM

4 ounces (116 g) CANDIED LEMON*, chopped fine

ICING SUGAR, sifted

CREME ANGLAISE (recipe below)

Preheat the oven to 385° F (200° C). Brush insides of the soufflé molds with melted butter and swirl sugar inside to coat. Combine the pastry cream, egg yolks, and candied lemon. Whip the egg whites until stiff and fold into the pastry cream. Fill molds to the brim and bake for 12 minutes. Dust tops with icing sugar and serve with creme anglaise on the side.

Crème anglaise:

4 EGG YOLKS

⅓ cup (80 ml) WHITE SUGAR

1 ½ cups (375 ml) WHOLE MILK

½ teaspoon (2.5 ml) VANILLA EXTRACT

In a heavy saucepan, combine the egg yolks and the sugar, beating until thick and lemon-coloured. Add the milk in slowly, beating well. Put over a low heat and stir constantly until custard is slightly thickened. It should coat a wooden spoon. Add the vanilla extract to complete.

* CANDIED LEMON is available in any baking speciality section of your local supermarket.

Top Ten Customer Comments

1. Thanks for the great party. My friends like to come to the Tomato because you really care about kids. You really like us.
 – *Your Tomato Pal, Elisa, age 9*
 (*Note: The Tomato now has "Tomato Pal" postcards and patches, thanks to Elisa.*)

2. Yippie yio yay! Tomato chow on a rainy day. Yum!
 – *A Farmer*

3. Finding the washroom is easy. It's like walking down the Yellow Brick Road. All you have to do is count five red squares and remember that you're walking through Momma Tomato's kitchen. It may not be the Land of Oz, but it's definitely a place you have to see. – *Anonymous*

4. I tried to buy some gum. You don't sell gum. Thanks, anyway.
 – *Chris Hooper, Venice, California*

5. Oogie oogie wow wow wow! Great gazpacho! – *Anonymous*

6. I just sat down and looked up at this wonderful arrangement of orchids in front of this austere backdrop of branches. Absolutely great. It made my stay a lot more delightful.
 – *Robert*

7. Diane, I love your place so much! I hope I'm ready when my daughter Anna tempts me to open a café, just as you were when Jennifer came to you with the idea of the Tomato.
 – *Bonnie Stern, Toronto, Ontario Cookbook Author*

8. Your meel was good. i didn't have muck though.
 – *Anonymous Youngster*

9. Let's see. I think your customers are, hmm, well, pretty good. I like the hat on that man over there. And the woman behind me has a nice laugh. Sometimes your customers are really yuppie. I see them traipsing in from their fancy Jags. Hey, but that's okay. It brings some cheerful, creative energy to our neighbourhood. – *Anonymous*

10. I like your customers. They're a lot better than the art, that's for sure! By the way, I love the visit through the kitchen to the bathroom. – *Anonymous*

Index

"This book is bound
"Repkover" to lay
flat when opened".